I0390735

CONTENTS

Cover image: Boris Ostrerov

WERKS issue 2, 2019. Interviews, reviews, and design by David Downs. Images provided by the artists. All content © David Downs and Sprocketbox Publishing 2019 All Rights Reserved. For information about WERKS publication please contact: sprocketbox@gmail.com

KELLEY JOHNSON

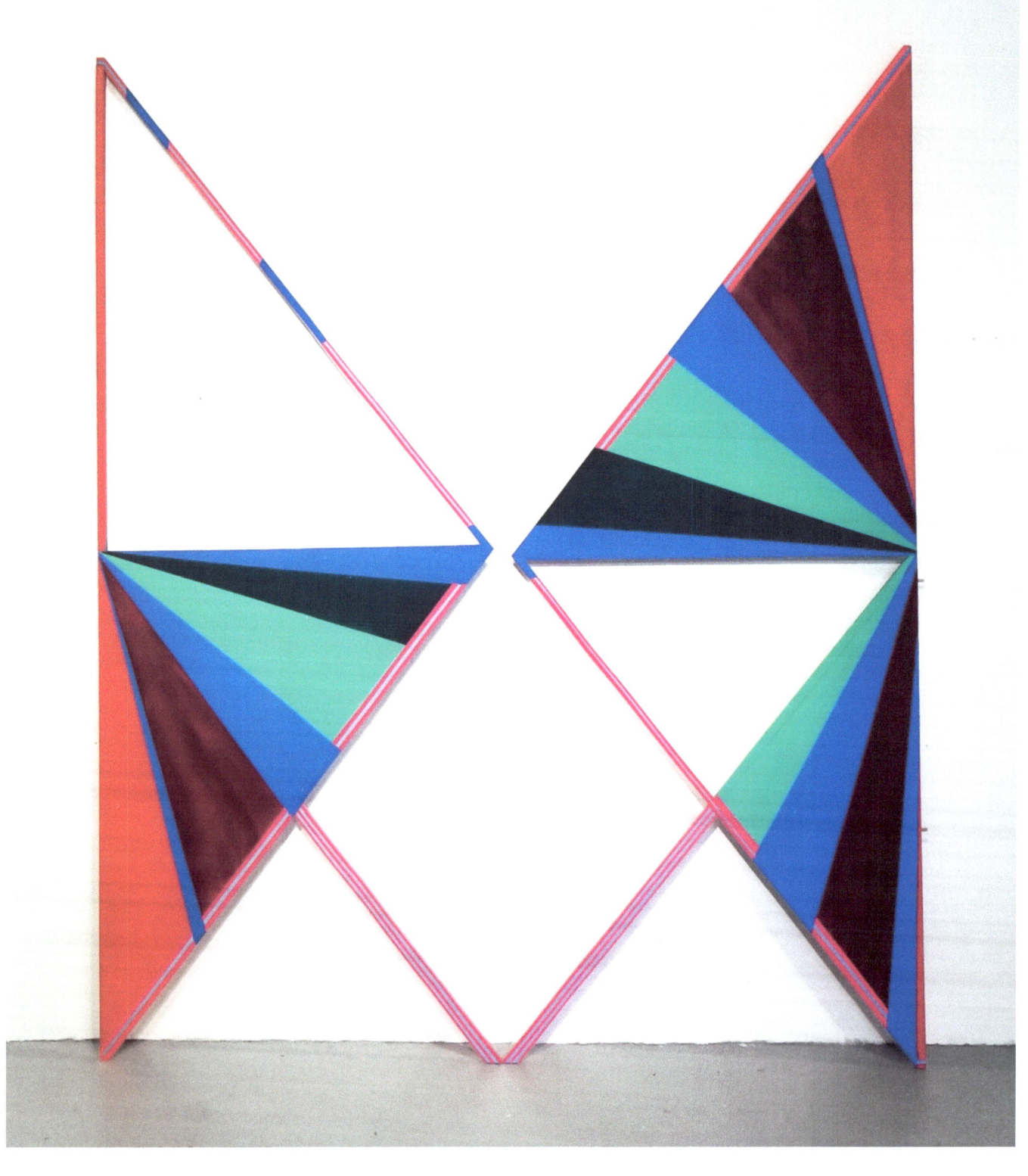

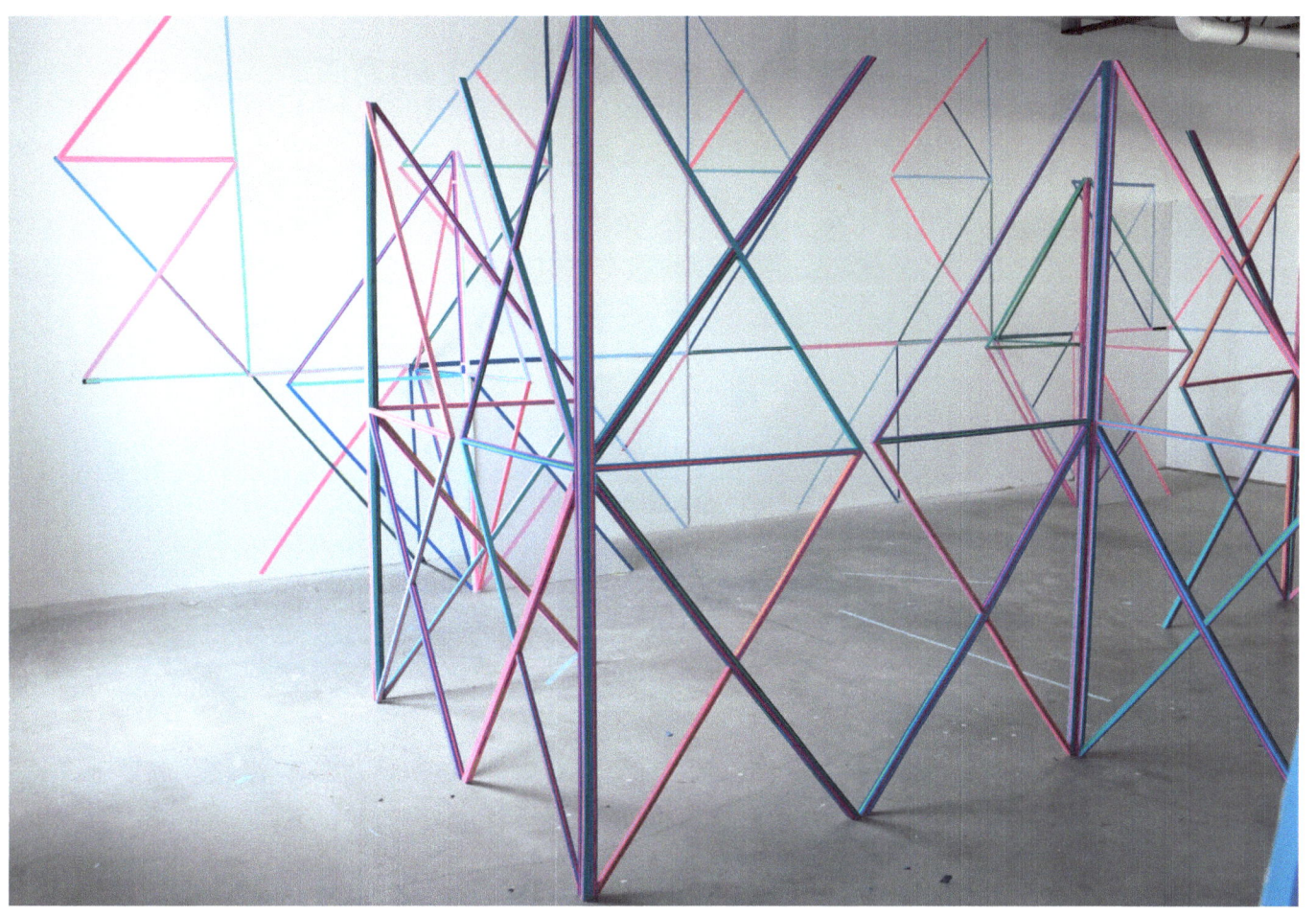

WERKS: You have a very large body of work throughout which is a running theme of geometric patterns created by intersecting lines of various materials. When did you start working in these motifs? What do they mean for you personally?

Kelley Johnson: I started off as a figurative/observational painter. Later I realized that what I was doing at the time was painting my position in space, in a way. It was almost a documentation of seeing from a specific view point; an interaction between painter and the translation of observed information onto the two dimensional plane. I noticed that for the viewer, the work was always a little distant. Looking into the "window" but not really having much of a physical interaction with the work. I think of the new work as an interactive painting. A physical interaction with space that adjusts and changes based on the viewers own position. It was still addressing formal concerns of space both 2 and 3D, like a living painting. I think that time, or our relationship with time and space are typically taken for granted. We are constantly thinking about the past or future while rarely living in the moment or even being aware of our surroundings.

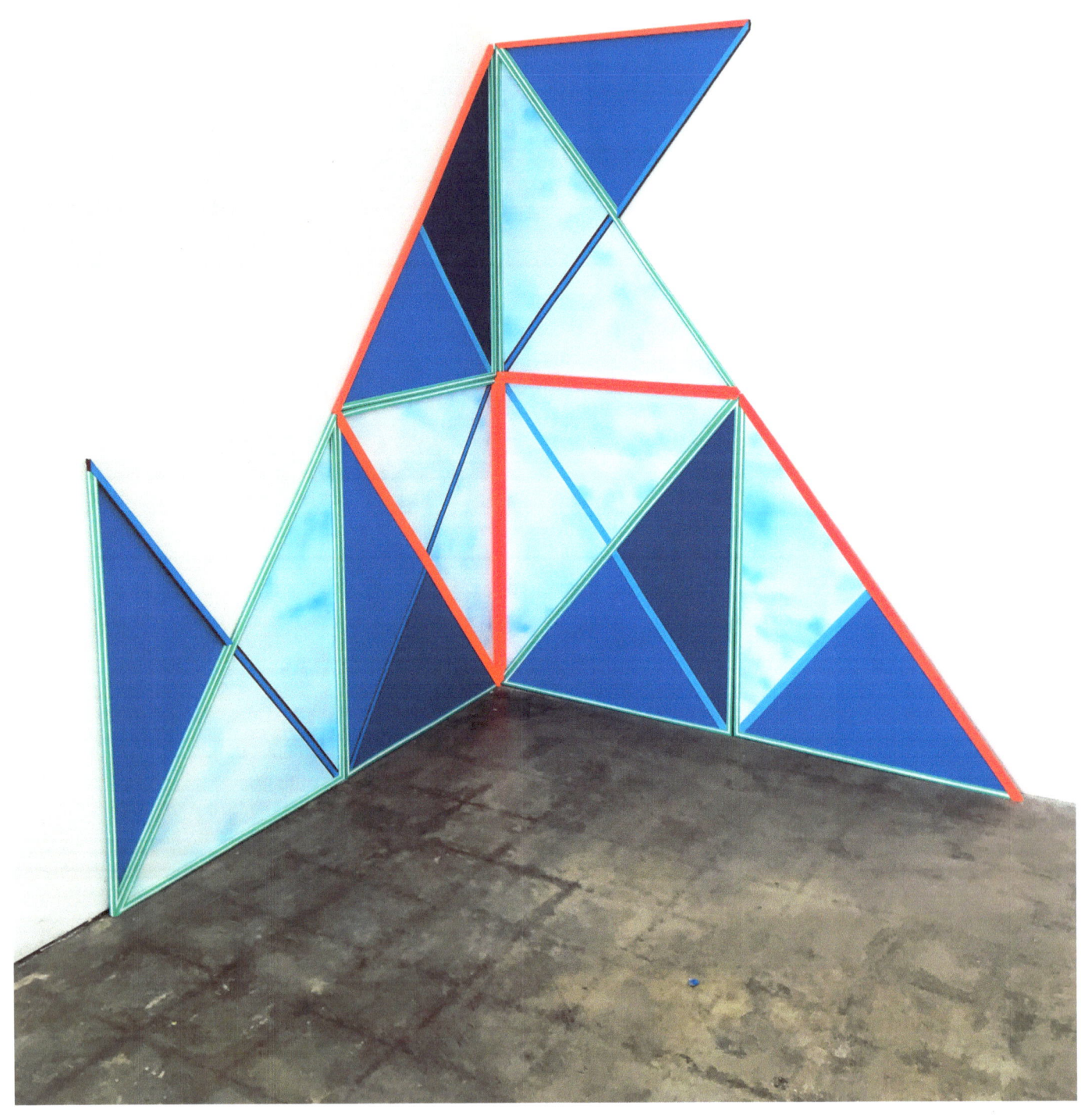

I think painters have always been interested in paintings doing things that they can't do, like making an awareness of time. I'm looking for a direct physical interaction with painting and creating an awareness of time and space and our position within it.

W: On your Instagram you give us a view of what you're working on and how you figure things out. It seems that you create mock-ups of the structures that you intend to build. What materials are using for the mock ups? Can you take them apart? Are they interchangeable? Do you use the same materials

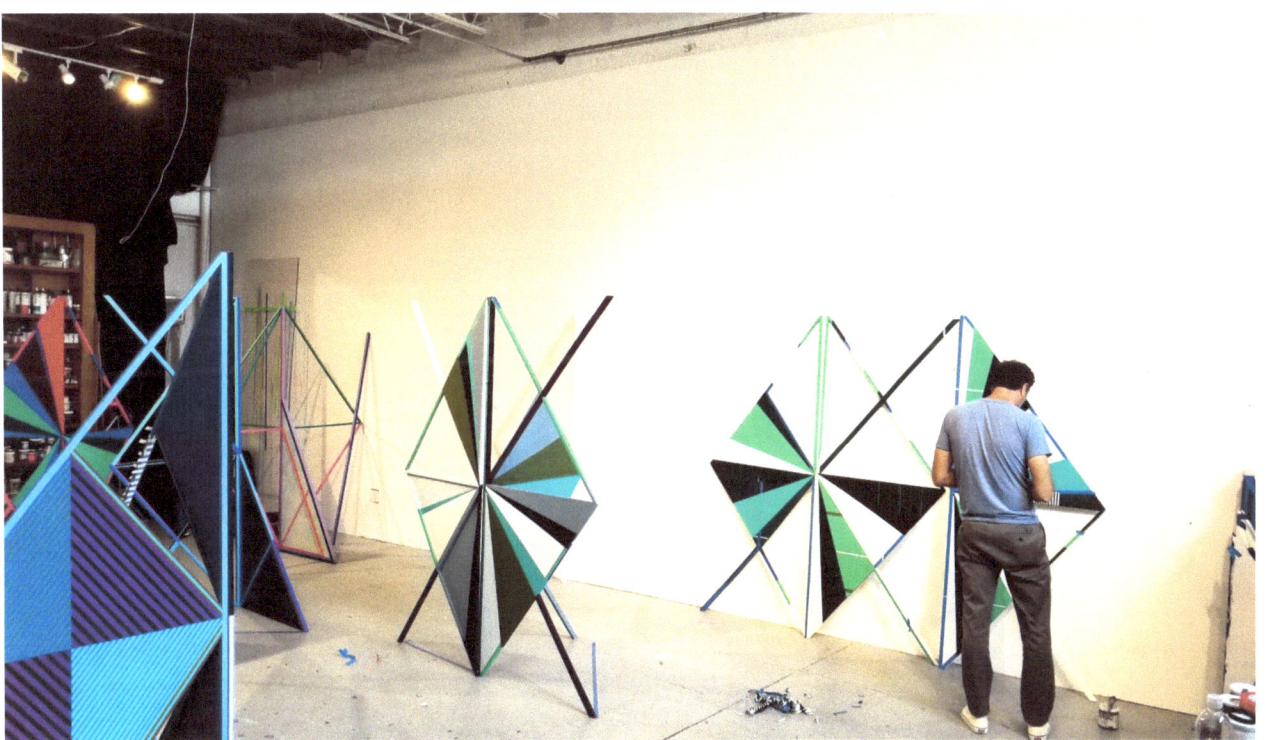

when you create the final installation?

KJ: I start off using a repetitive mark or shape that typically evolves into a pattern. The pattern helps to establish a structural framework or at set of rules that start the painting/building process. From this point the works evolve in an intuitive way, but usually still containing at least a part of the initial framework. So its kind of a loose structure to work from that allows the dimensions and shape of the works to unfold in an organic way. Hopefully allowing for a dialogue between two and three dimensional space.

With a lot of the 3-D and installation work I start off with 1x1 inch PVC or wood, usually 8 foot long, that I cut along with wood or PVC panels. Lately I have been making repetitive shapes that fit together with one another.
Usually the beginning is quite messy and things are stuck together with tape. Eventually the structures become more apparent and things start to become precise in the way it's constructed. At this point color and form are beginning a dialogue that will inform how the work will read, but nothing is final until the end. I like to think of this way of working as drawing or painting in space. At first the sketch is quite messy but becomes more refined with an internal logic by the end.

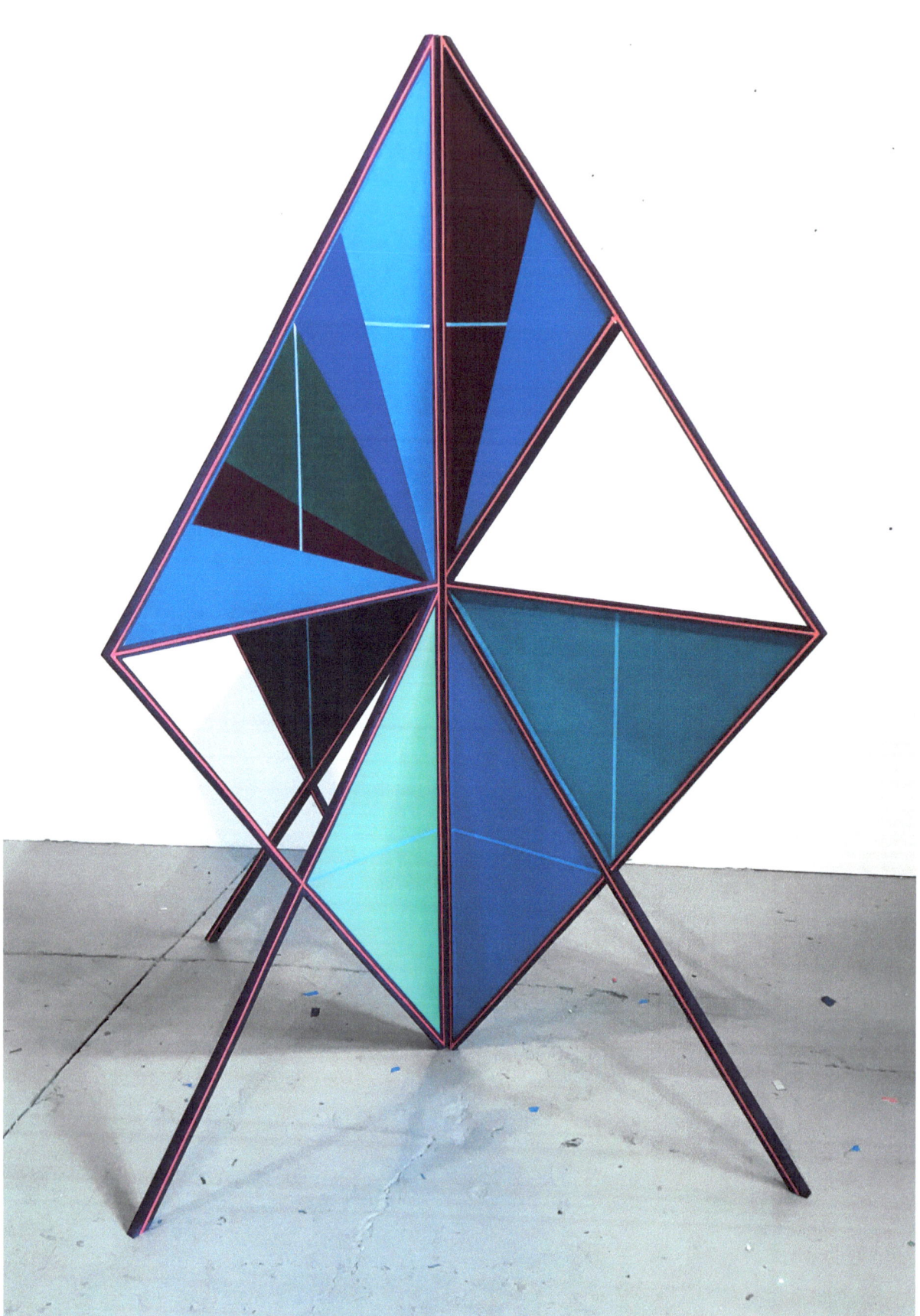

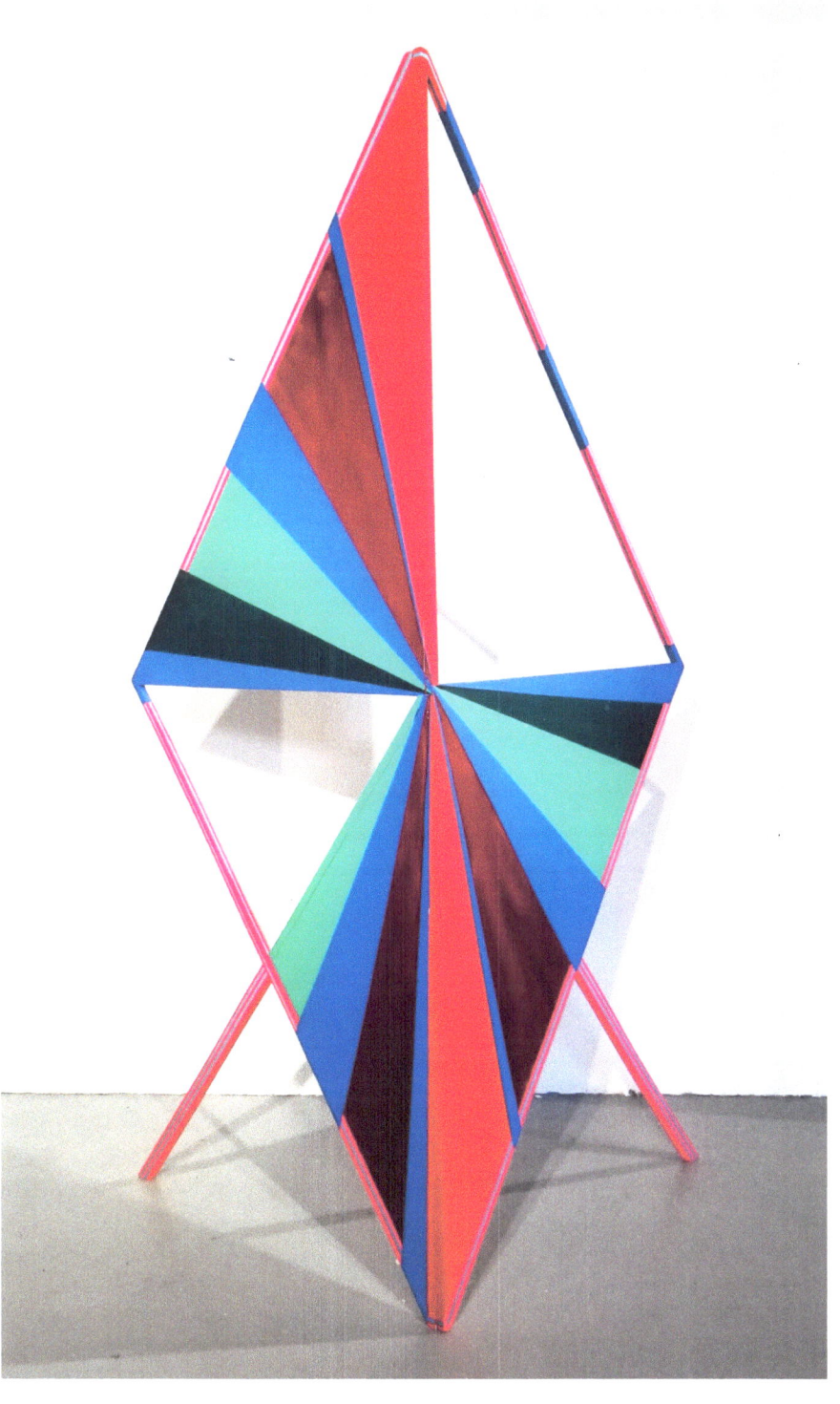

W: What is your goal with the structures you are building? Besides being aesthetically captivating, what type of ideas and concepts are you working with and what first influenced those ideas?

KJ: I want the viewer to interact with the structures both as paintings and sculptures. As if they entered the painted space. I always want painting to do things that it can't, like create an awareness of time and space both physical and optical, while doing so within the formal concerns of painting. I feel like we are so caught up in our day to day, fast paced digital world that we are forgetting how to interact with the physical world, or really slowing down, breathing and walking through space while being in the present moment. Not thinking about the past or future.

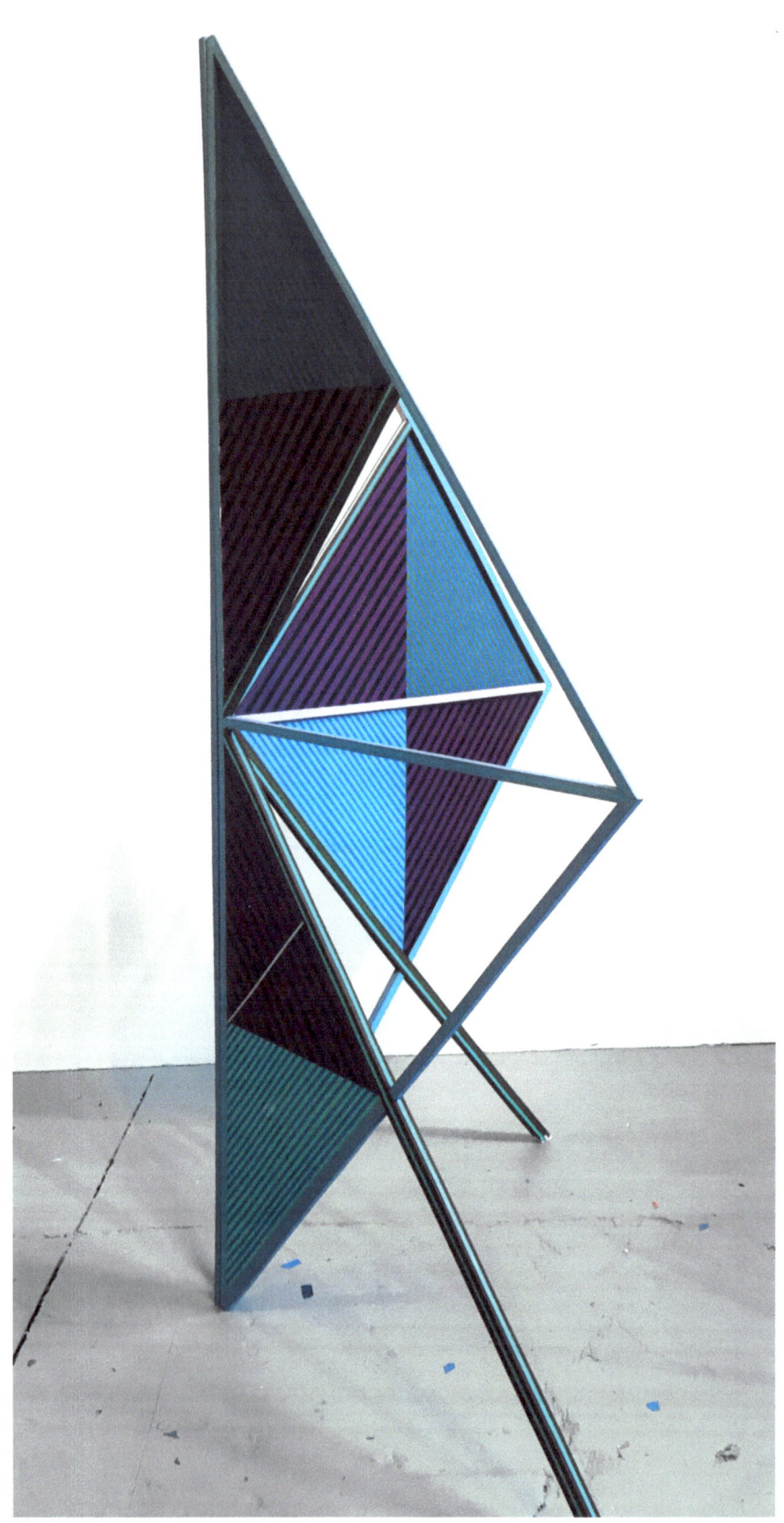

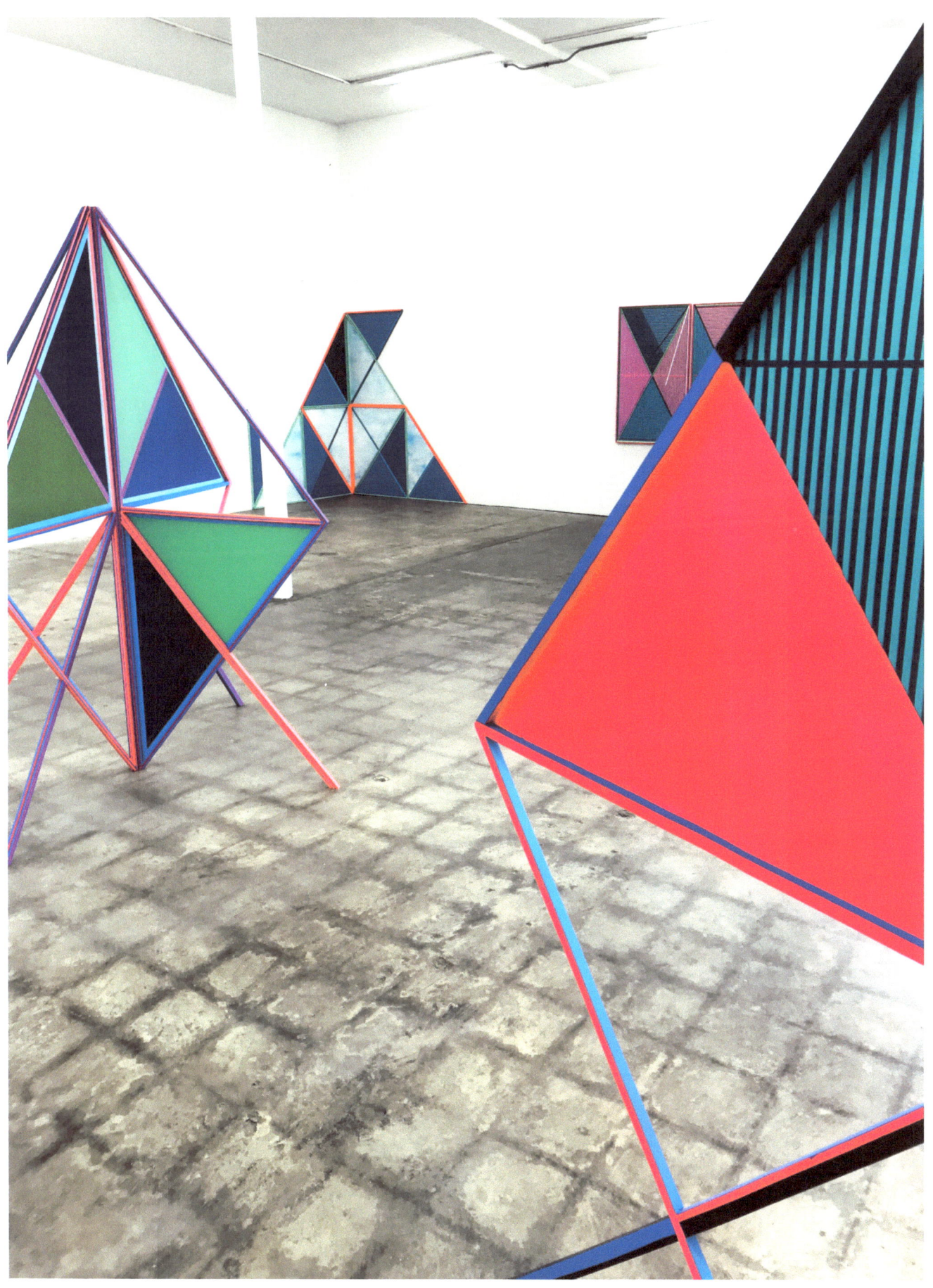

Megan Bickel

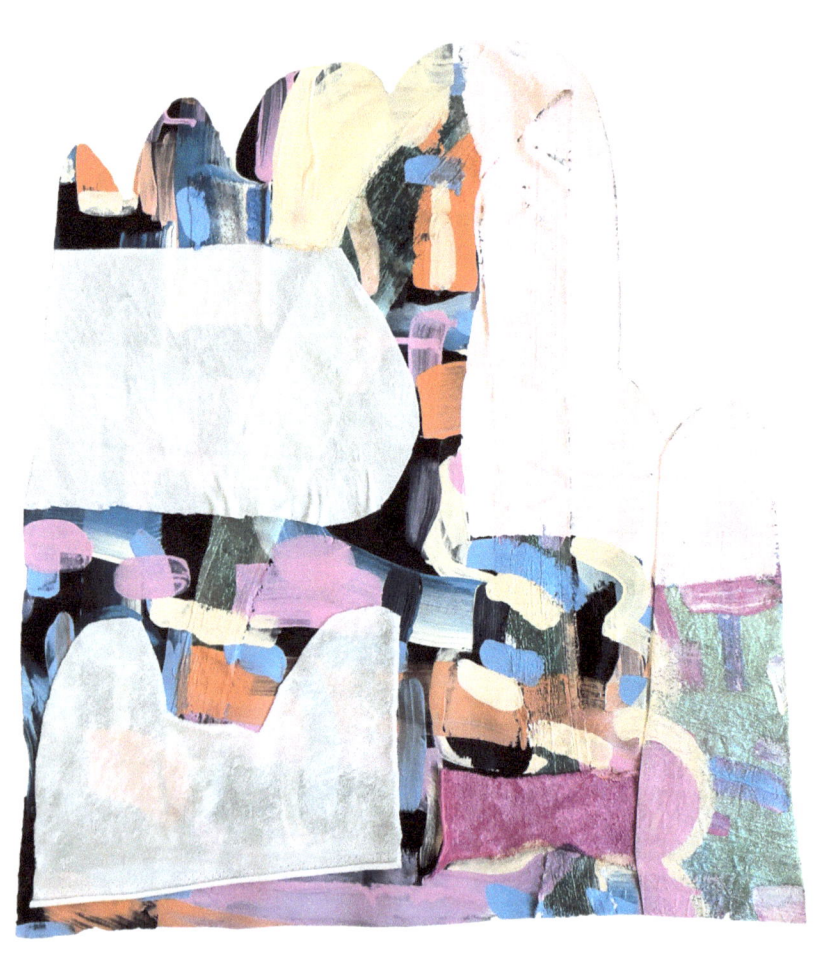

WERKS: The first thing that caught my attention about your work was the nontraditional materials of which you are creating images, painted fabric and maybe other things and the decisions you've made about how to display the work. The theory behind the work is also interesting, and we will definitely dive into that later. For now however, let's talk about the physical nature of the paintings. Can you tell us about the materials you are using and how you make decisions on how to assemble them? I feel the process relates formally to painting but delves into sculpture and assemblage.

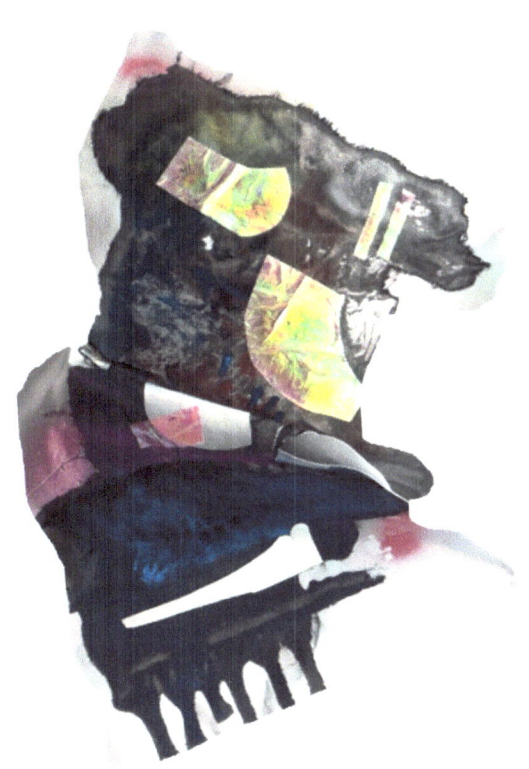

Megan Bickel: I mean, the answer is in the question, right? If I wanted to be brief I could just say that I'm bored of making paintings, but not painting. So I'm making these objects that don't really feel like they fit anywhere. But that makes for a boring interview.

I feel obligated to preface my answer with an explanation of the steps that got me to this point, stylistically. In the fall of last year I began to feel very discontent with painting. For me, it felt like a one-sided relationship in which I was pouring energy and getting nothing back. The work felt really flat, disengaged, and frankly boring— they had no argumentativeness to them. I had played around with painting and collaging drawings on transparency paper and utilizing epoxy resins for depth; playing around with the transparency that those materials' provided. One day I had some silk layering around because I was experimenting with textile wallpaper ideas and I wanted to see what would happen if I loosely placed some fabric,

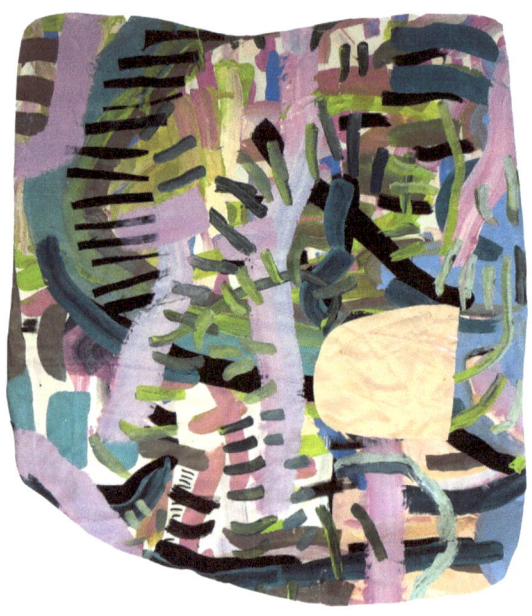

drawings, and transparency paper together and painted on them—just some intuitive patterned mark-making. I found the creation of literal space in these paintings to be the half-answer to what I was frustrated with. Long story short, it went through several stages and then landed where it is now.

I approach these works as paintings in that they are born on a stretcher, and I work on them while they are on a wall, and I of course paint them. They become assembled when I begin taking other paintings and cutting them apart and adhering them to the painting I'm currently developing. I also practice cutting fabric or paintings in a way that replicates the types of mark making that I employ—in an effort to visually and texturally confuse the visual space and surface that I'm simulating. I use the act of painting to *simulate* space while I utilize textiles, glitter, sequins and other things as surfaces to activate the surface of the painting as an object. One is about the act of representation and one is about the creation of a thing— or about reduction and addition, I'm not really sure. No matter the subject matter, my work always subjectively references juxtaposition or tension, so it makes sense that I would also employ that idea in the physical creation of work. I'm really enjoying velvet currently because, in all of its plasticity; when you apply paint to it, it begins to physically feel like a scab. Its texturally fleshy and human in that way. Hard and crunchy, but appearing to maintain its softness, it creates confusion—it's misleading.

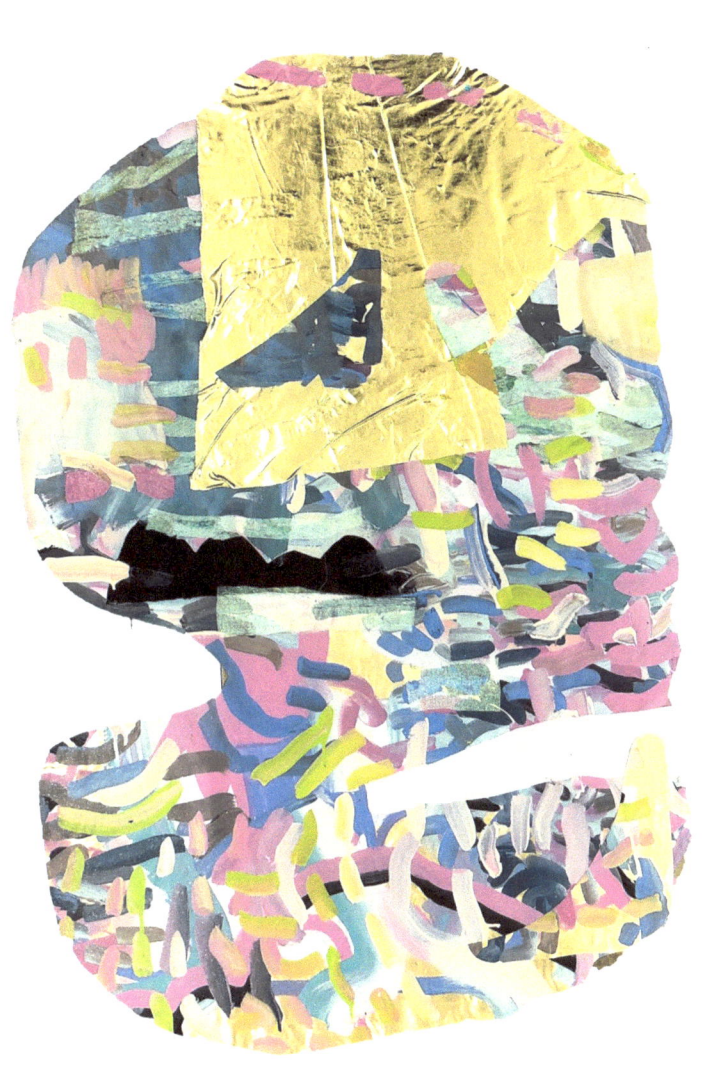

In regards to how I install the paintings: altering spaces has long been a tradition of architecture, post-conceptual installation, and sculpture, but I'm curious as to how I can try (key word, there) to add to that conversation utilizing two-dimensional painting. I'm curious in attempting to see if it's possible to disrupt the two-dimensionality of painting by removing them from the wall and stretcher and molding the fabric in such a way that it's also no longer flat, whilst referencing the history of that type of object by continuing to utilize wallhangings. Wall surface visually recalls the history of painting and interacting with the "wall" as a space. I guess, in terms of their presentation, I'm trying to confuse the space the viewer finds themselves in, while upholding some tradition to two-dimensional painting.

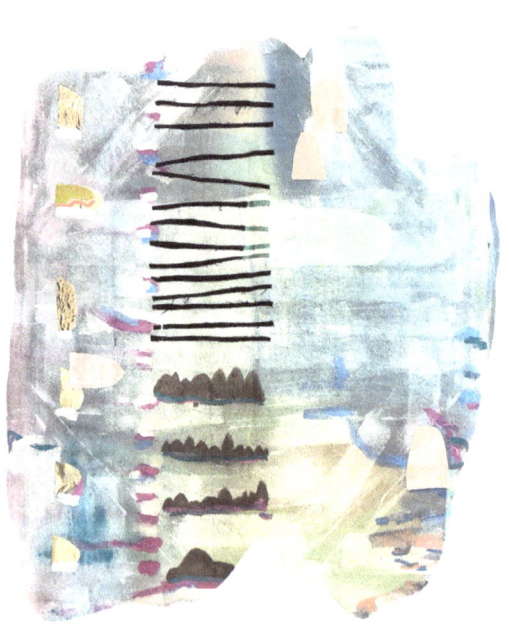

W: What is it about the tradition of painting that makes you want to reference it? It's something a lot of painters do, including myself, and might not be impossible to avoid as a painter, but I often wonder why it's important for the objects we create to be paintings at all. For you, what is it that ties you strongly to that medium?

MB: This is a really good question, and one that gave me some serious pause. Perhaps its the case that if we studied painting or art history anytime after 1980, we were collectively effected by the results of Postmodernism and there by feel the need to constantly reference the history of painting in order to validate our own act of painting.

I don't think that I want to reference it, so much as understand that I'm contributing to a craft that dates to prehistory. You can't make a painting without understanding your context or your place. For me, my context includes my gender, issues with my mental health, political views, geographic location, perception of the world (effected by my past experiences), and of course my education, and so its inescapable. As far as what ties me to painting. . . God, I really don't have an answer for that. It's my fall back and probably where my strengths are? There's safety

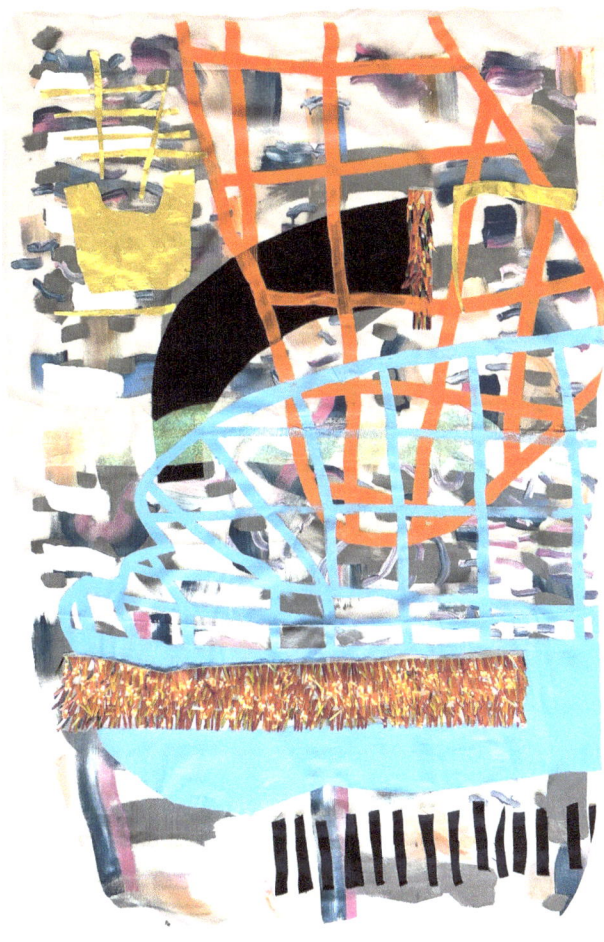

in it? I can try to discuss whatever I want and at the end of the day everyone knows a painting when they see one and nothing else matters? Perhaps, even though I'm working through ideas that take a load of explaining, I want something to be recognizable, for the audience and myself? I really don't know. . .

W: I think you're definitely right in that, in the end, people can recognize it as a painting no matter what is being discussed by the work. That can be a good thing as it creates an entry point for people to look deeper into the work. You mentioned geographic location. How would you say that affects your work?

MB: Well, to clarify, within the context of the previous question I was just stating that my location within the world is a contributing factor to how I take in information and thus, make work. I wouldn't say that it effects the work directly, but perhaps indirectly, accidentally, or in some circuitous way that I'm unaware of at the moment.

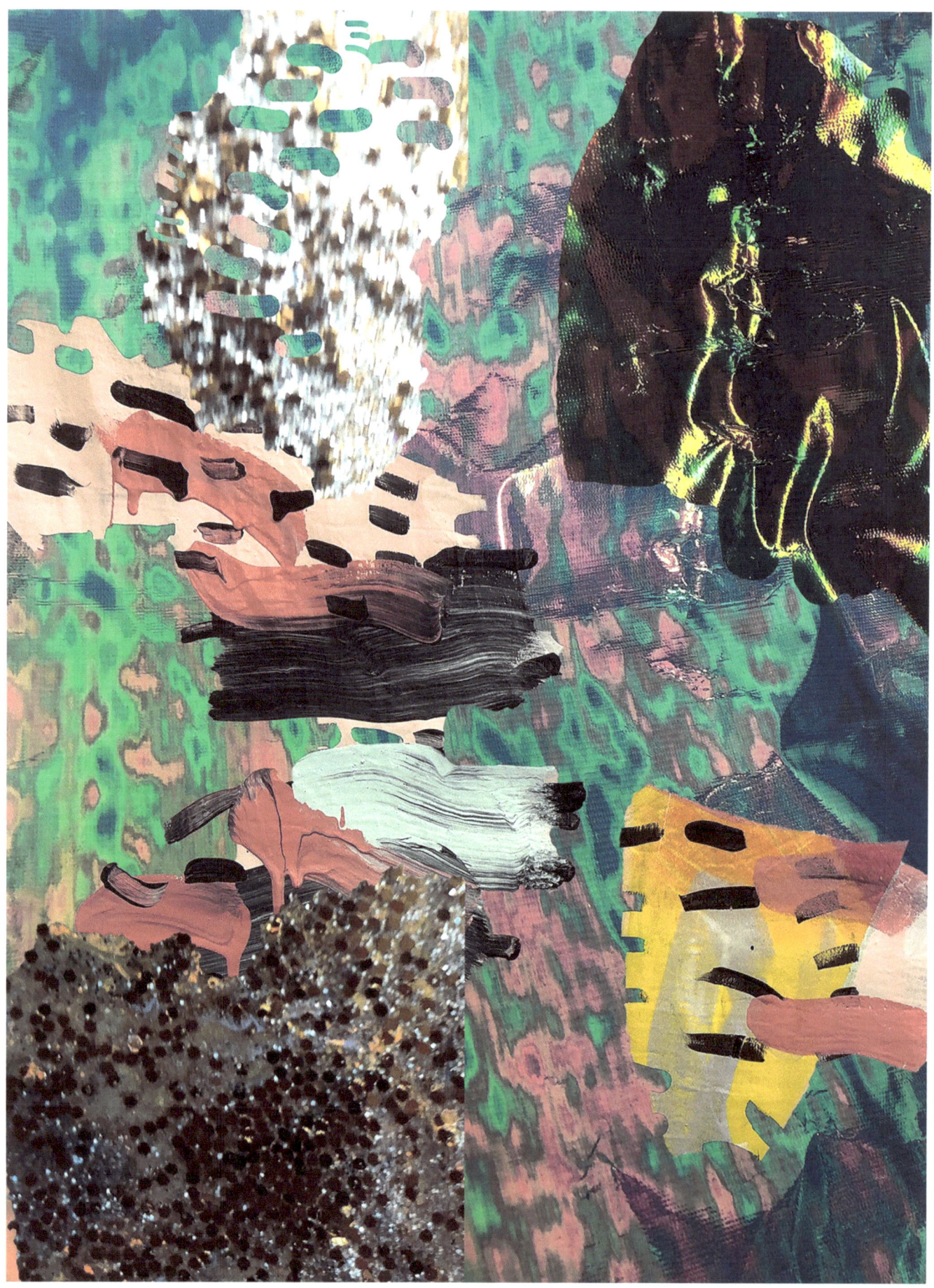

I will say though, that being located in Louisville, Kentucky, as opposed to a bigger city, is an interesting position as an artist. Louisville has a very large creative community considering its overall population, a very art positive local government, and hasn't (yet) been hit by the housing / commercial market shortage that a lot of cities are facing right now. So it's pretty cost effective to live and operate here--which of course grants me the biggest requirement that artists are always short on--time, as well as a little bit of financial flexibility despite a very modest income. All of which are factors that obviously impact my ability to make work, travel to exhibitions / residencies, or take other opportunities.

W: In your artist statement you talk about PTSD induced depression and the art process seems therapeutic for you in a way as a sort of intellectual rationalization of your feelings. Does the work ever directly correlate to specific events or is it more of an intertwining of multiple, less distinguishable events?

MB: This is an idea I'm consistently working through as I strongly discourage work that is therapeutic. I don't think painting should be a therapy session. That being said, you would be correct in finding that it is therapeutic when you can distance yourself and historicize your own trauma. When I'm on the outside of a depressive episode, my depression and coping mechanisms associated with trauma are objectively interesting to me; but they certainly aren't specific to me or my experiences.

I would say that I'm not trying to work through specific events because I don't think that I am at a point where I could submerge myself into those thoughts and maintain productivity; but rather working through the ways that those events affected me, or working through my reactions to new experience that are obviously effected by my previous experiences.

W: What are some things you're looking forward to this fall or beyond? Do you have any shows coming up?

I just began working towards my MFA; so that's pretty exciting.
Artist interview in 10011 Mag (No3), out of NY and associated with Claudia Eng Gallery -- recently published
University of Louisville MFA Exhibition (dates tba) located at the freshly minted MFA / Faculty Studio Facility
Erie Gallery--Erie, Pennsylvania (early 2019, dates tbd)
The Good American, a Two-Person Exhibition with Noah Howard and Darrin Milliner-- houseguest gallery, louisville KY (curated by me opening Sept 14-Nov3rd)

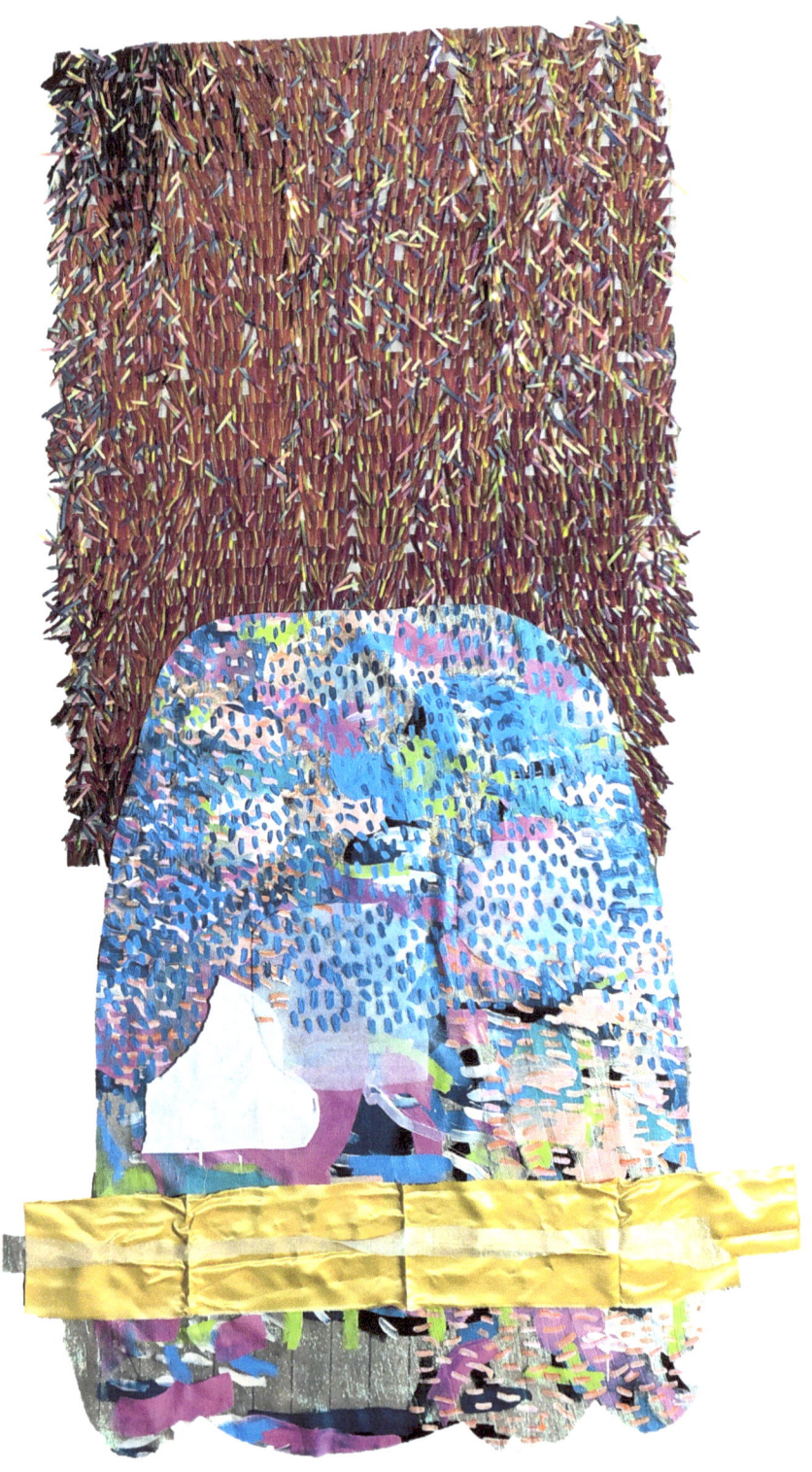

AARON SCHEER

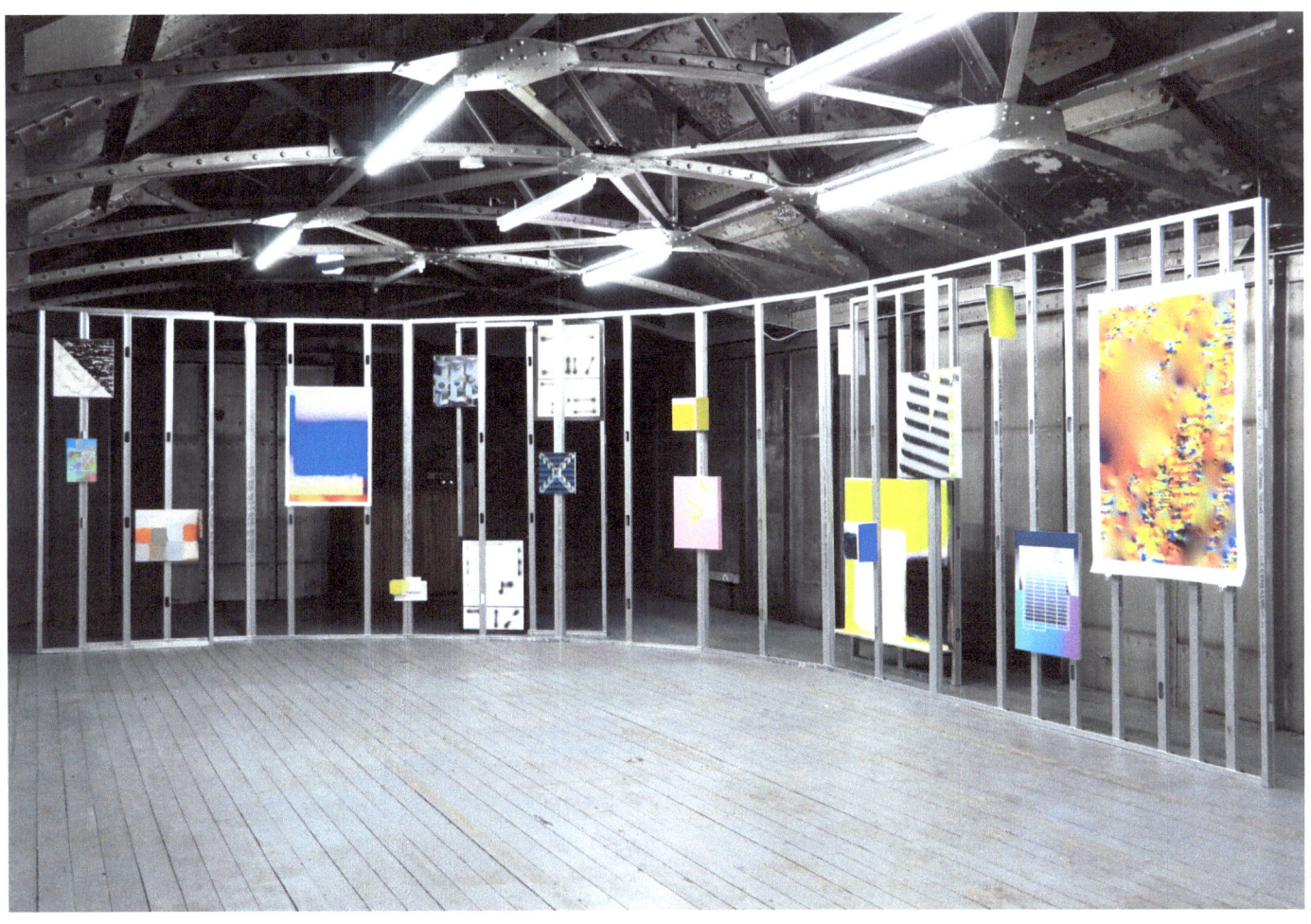

Werks: We had the honor of publishing a few of your artworks and our first issue in the spring. The theme of that work seems to be related to the digital realm, but there are references to a physical medium being used. Can you tell us a little bit about the materials used in your work?

Aaron Scheer: Sure. As you said, my works are related to the digital realm. Having said that, I am still wandering between the digital and the analog. My work is a hybrid. A hybrid of virtual and physical inspiration. A hybrid of working with digital and analog techniques. A hybrid of showcasing my works in online and physical spaces. And a hybrid of using tangible and intangible matter.

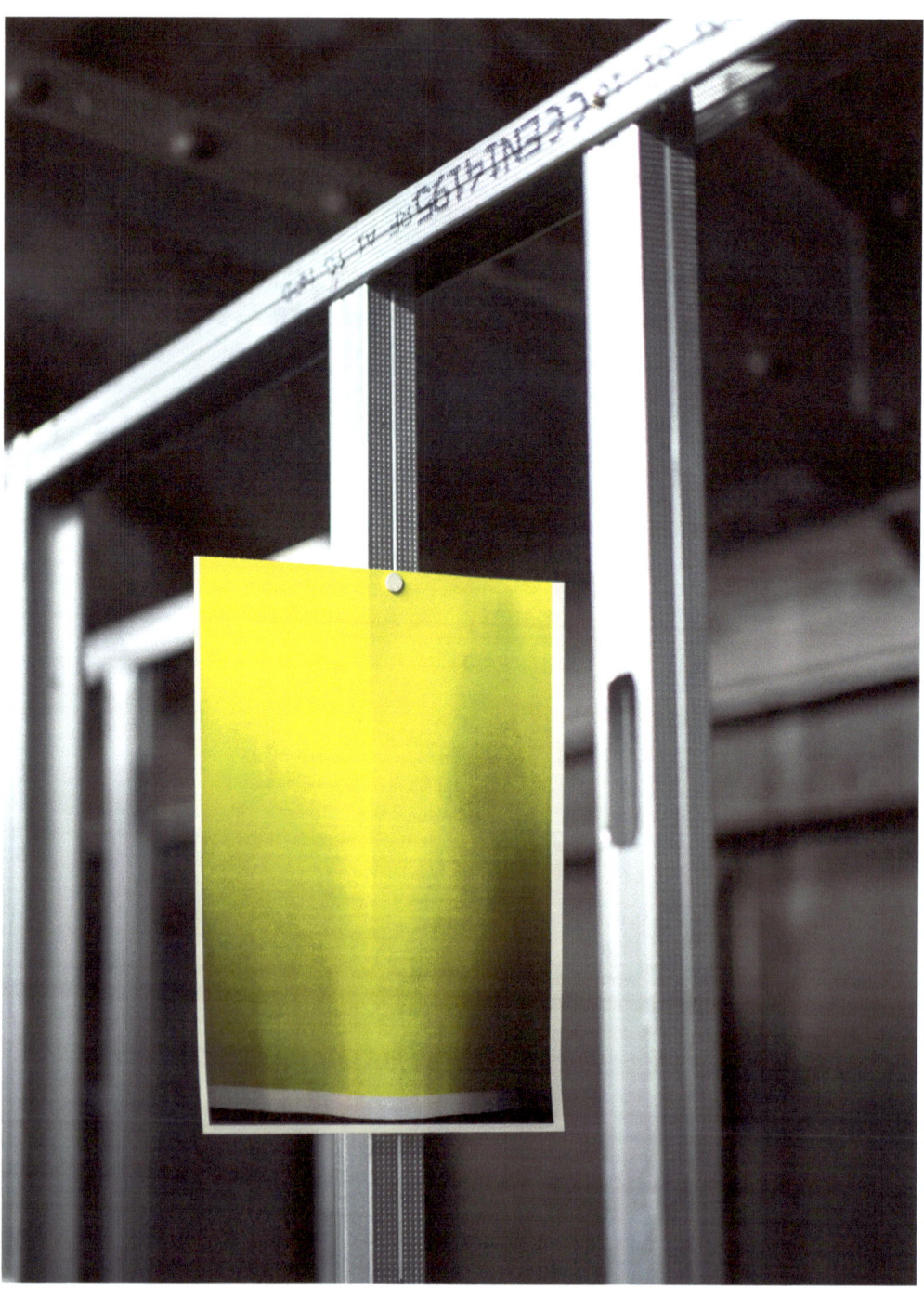

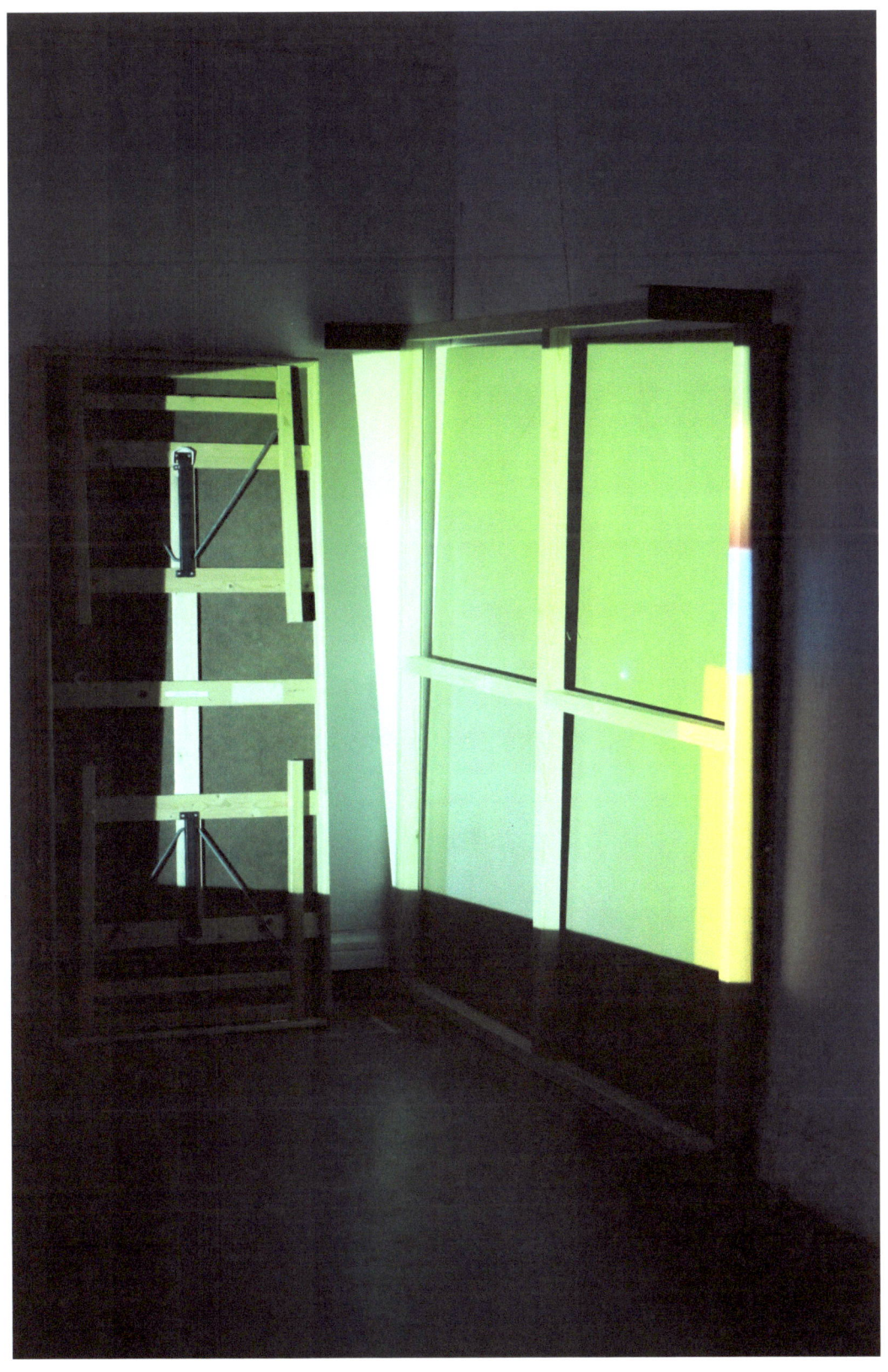

To answer your question, I am a lot experimenting with digital material such as screenshots of pixelated music videos, blurred images of post-its, or closeups of late night adventures. Another pool of digital painting material is the internet. Sometimes I just surf randomly through the web, or come across something that I find interesting: colours, compositions, content; whatever it is. I use what is instantly accessible. I was always a fan of using the everyday in my work. In one way, or the other. Nevertheless, most of my digital paintings will be printed out on raw natural archival paper. It adds the last painterly attitude towards my digital paintings. The boundaries between what has been made with digital and analog techniques gets ultimately blurred. A boundary between virtual and physical reality. Additionally, I still use more classical material such as oil crayon, spray paint or oil paint. Sometimes, I throw everything in one pot and mix techniques and material.

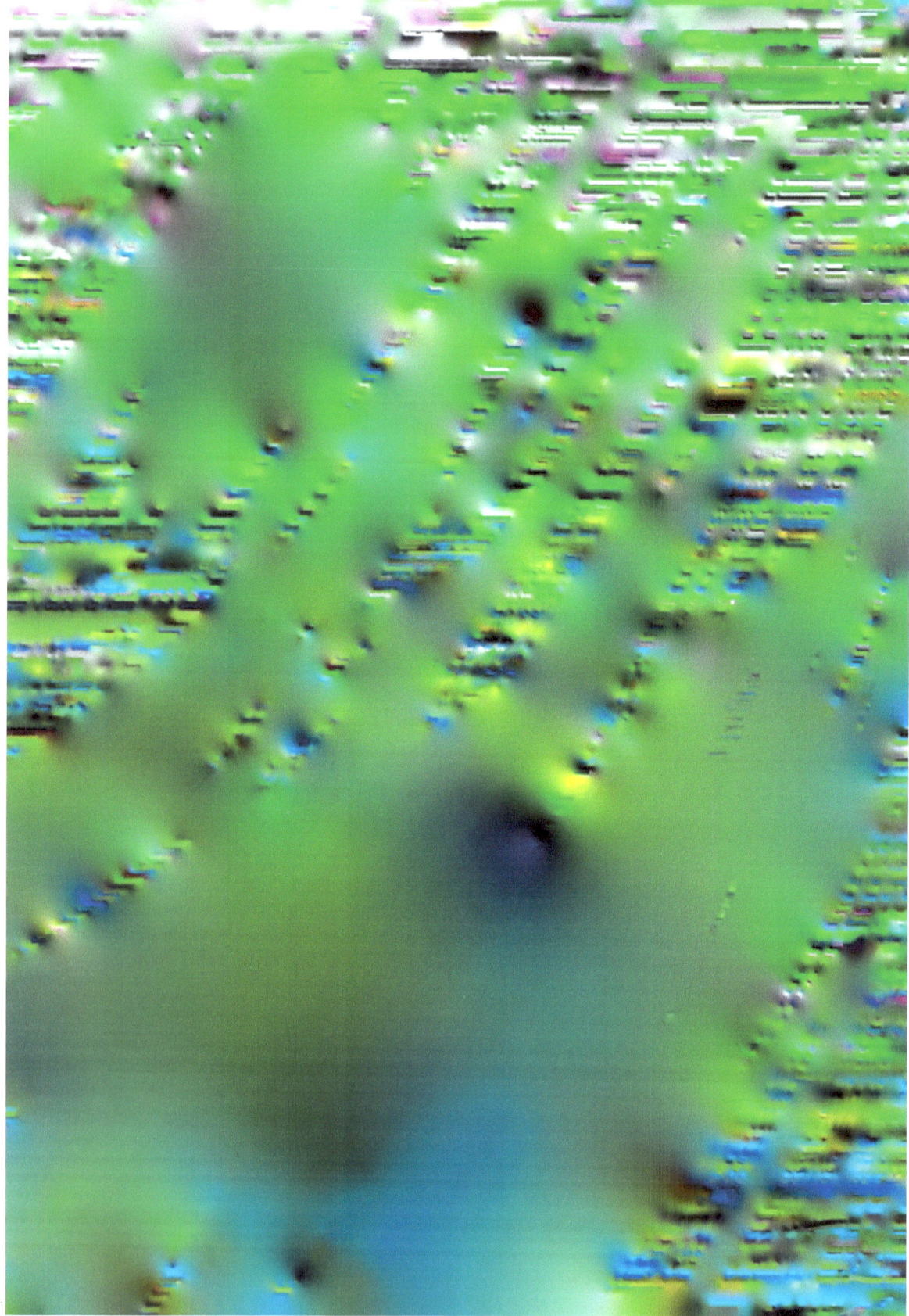

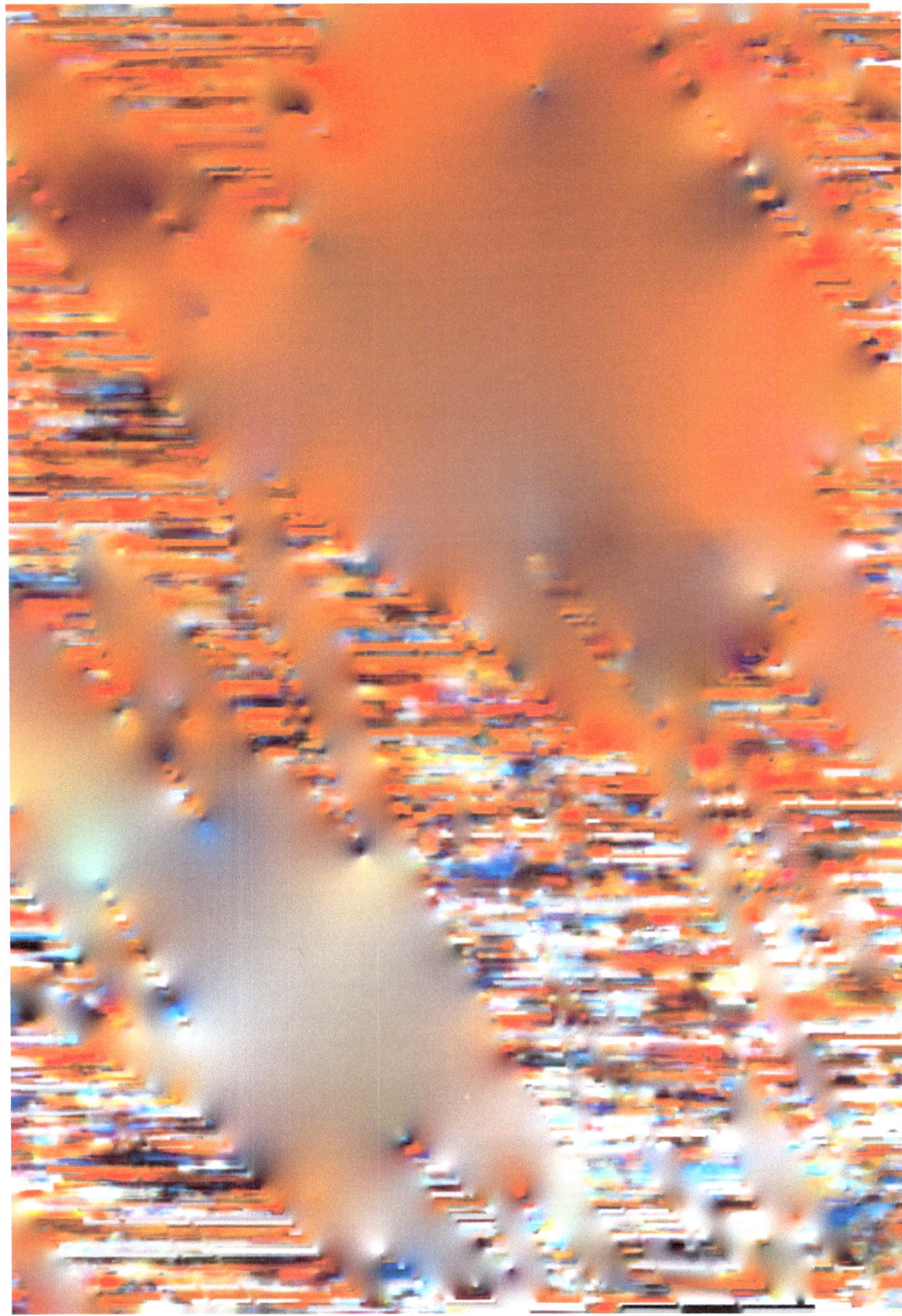

W: It sounds like you're taking the art of assemblage into the digital realm. What's interesting is what becomes of those images the way you use them. You've turned them into something completely separate from the original found image material. I was just thinking about how Joan Mitchell, for instance, didn't paint actual landscapes or objects that she remembered but rather the impression made on her, affected by her eidetic sensibilities. Are you using the images you find directly as one might make collage or are those images influencing you to make something separately?

AS: Joan Mitchell, love her bold and pioneering abstract and expressionist works. Reminds me of some of my father's works, who started out with abstract expressionist figuration and turned more and more towards pure abstraction later on.

My paintings though are a mix of collage of the original images and impressions of inspirational source material. I use both techniques. But you are right when saying that the final pieces are existing independently. What is important to understand is that I manipulate all images in one way or the other: by cutting them, zooming in to them, glitching them, blurring them, painting over them and so forth. Some of the material even becomes painting material comparable to oil paint or acrylic paint. Almost like a color palette that is smeared together and can be directly applied to the canvas or paper. Just that the canvas becomes the digital file.

What I'm looking for is essence. I'm in search for the atmospheric feeling of things. Things that can reveal deep emotions, which one can't explain, put in words. It's fascinating for me. Especially as I'm in other situations of life trying to look for clear rational verbal explanations (and even in this interview). I guess a lot of abstract artists are looking for some kind of metaphysical emotional reality, in various ways. Still, I do have some figurative references in my works, may it be Mac icons, or the Mac toolbar; or even more concrete ones like selfies and apps in my smartphone paintings.

W: When you talk about emotions, are you trying to create a space in which the viewer will experience their own emotions when confronted with your work, or are you trying to convey, through the work, emotions of your own? I realize you might also be doing both. The delineation between the two is a strange one. Another way to put it; are you infusing the works with your own emotions hoping that the viewer will pick up on them, or is the work detached from your own personal feelings but created in a way to conjure an emotional response from the viewer? Does that make sense?

AS: I think every piece of art is in one way or the other creating a space where one can experience their very own emotional response to the piece. Mine as well. What kind of emotions is very different from person to person. Surely, I'm using a specific aesthetic in my works composed of a certain sense of (digital) beauty. But at the same time my pieces are distorted and at times disturbing. There needs to be tension. Without contrast, or any kind of ambiguity, it's not interesting for me.

Surely, there are also parts of my personal emotional state in my works. That is much torn between the poles of positivity and negativity. I guess this is where the tension is coming from. Also, I'm someone who can't decide and rather prefers to integrate what doesn't seem to fit in the first place. For me, it's a way to create something new, something complex. Most people, especially nowadays look for clear and easy answers to get back a sense of direction and purpose. I was always bored by that. And also think that this is not how life works. But It's also needed, in order to move on, to go somewhere. A thin line of swaying between two different poles, once again.

W: I find it interesting when you say, "at times disturbing." Something so abstract should feel benign because of its lack of reference in the real world, but it's not. Somehow you've captured a shift in perspective that feels a bit strange and unnerving. What do you think it is that creates that experience for a viewer? When it happens in your work is it intentional from the start or is it something you discover during the process and attempt to exploit further?

It might be a bit strange. But it is exactly what creates the mentioned tension in my work. What makes it interesting for me. The majority of my pieces might be pleasing and comforting in the first place, mainly due to choice of color, form and light. The majority of viewers say they are beautiful. My pieces drag you in. They lull you in. Almost like a visual demagogue. But there's more to it, once you really get into the work. You'll find glitches. You'll find distortions. You'll find tumour-like deformations, almost organic. You'll find erosion. You'll find dialysis. Everything is cluttered and excessive. There are a lot of flaws in this seemingly superficial beauty. But there's harmony and positivity as well. It's a fragile construction. A fragile ecosystem of colours, forms, light and references to a more and more technology-driven society.

There's a certain intention to it, but it comes very natural. All of my pieces somehow play with comfort and discomfort, positivity and negativity. That's a conscious decision. How it will manifest itself is left open during the process. It emerges. You just have to keep going. Reflect and act along the way. Radical trial and error. My works are very ambiguous. When it comes to their medium, their visual language or project statement. It reflects a deeper level of being: I'm not utopian, neither dystopian. It's more complex than that. And art gives me the chance to communicate that complexity, in my own way.

W: Obviously there's a lot of editing and manipulation in your images, but how does it usually start? Is there an image you find to begin with or do you start with just a blank screen and an idea?
AS: Starting point can be any inspiration source. A screenshot of a pixelated Big Bang Theory in between scenes banner while watching the series, a picture of the Burning Man on the internet, an interesting article about the Whole Earth Catalogue

and its relation to Silicon Valley gurus, a blurred snapshot made with my iPhone or testing out a new tool on Preview or Photoshop. So starting point can be anything from a random coincident to some more conscious research and experimentation. The experiments then grow organically from there. At one point, the experimentation process starts on the "digital canvas", which is in fact a blank white digital file that has a certain size. The digital counterpart to the analog canvas, or paper that I used to work with when I was younger. If you wish to say so, it is a rather traditional process of crafting a painting. Just that I do it mainly with the means of digital tools and sources.

Erin Hayden

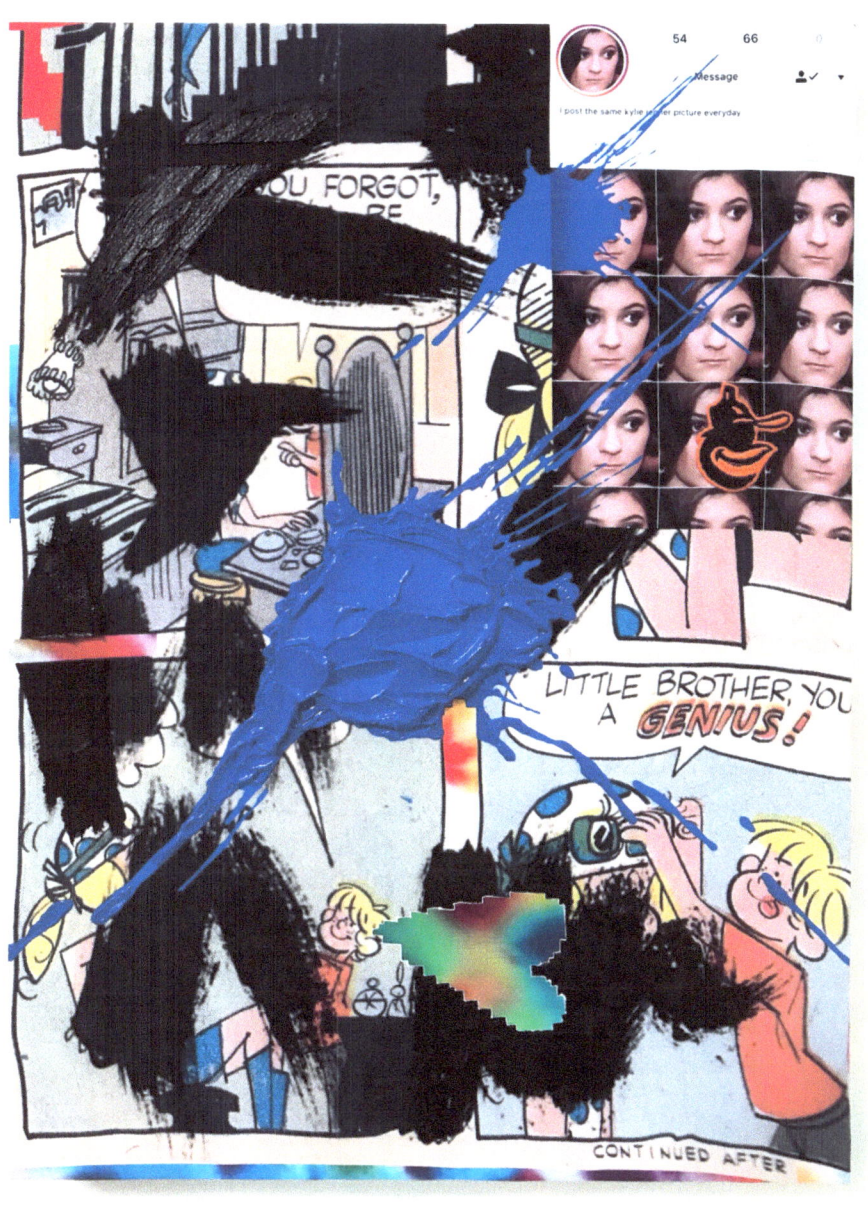

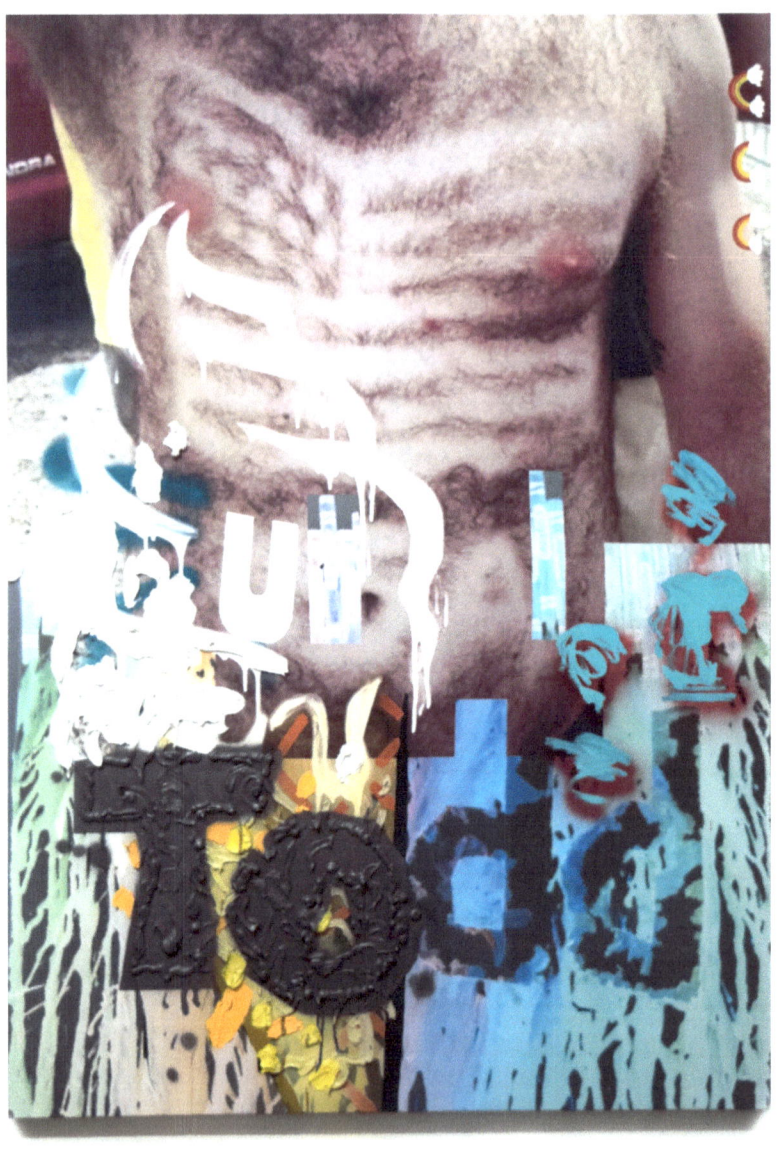

My studio practice makes use of both digitally and physically generated images, as well as performance and creative writing, to examine the intersection between modes of making most readily associated with the work of hobbyist or commercial artists and those of the contemporary fine art world.

In my paintings, I seek to locate a shared space between the digital world of the screen and the physical world of the hand-made mark. I create a back-and-forth play between images generated both digitally and in paint, allowing each medium to communicate both against and through the language of the other. In this way, painted areas may pronounce their physicality through fluid, painterly gestures or thick, impasto paint, or they may take on the hard edge, flat, and cold look of a digital graphic. Similarly, digitally printed images may assert their graphic origins, or they may, through digital manipulation, take on the appearance of painterly production. A deeper engagement is thus required to disentangle the painted from the printed. Ultimately, my concern with these works is not with the effects of technology on the life of images, but with the effects of technological advancements on our lives.

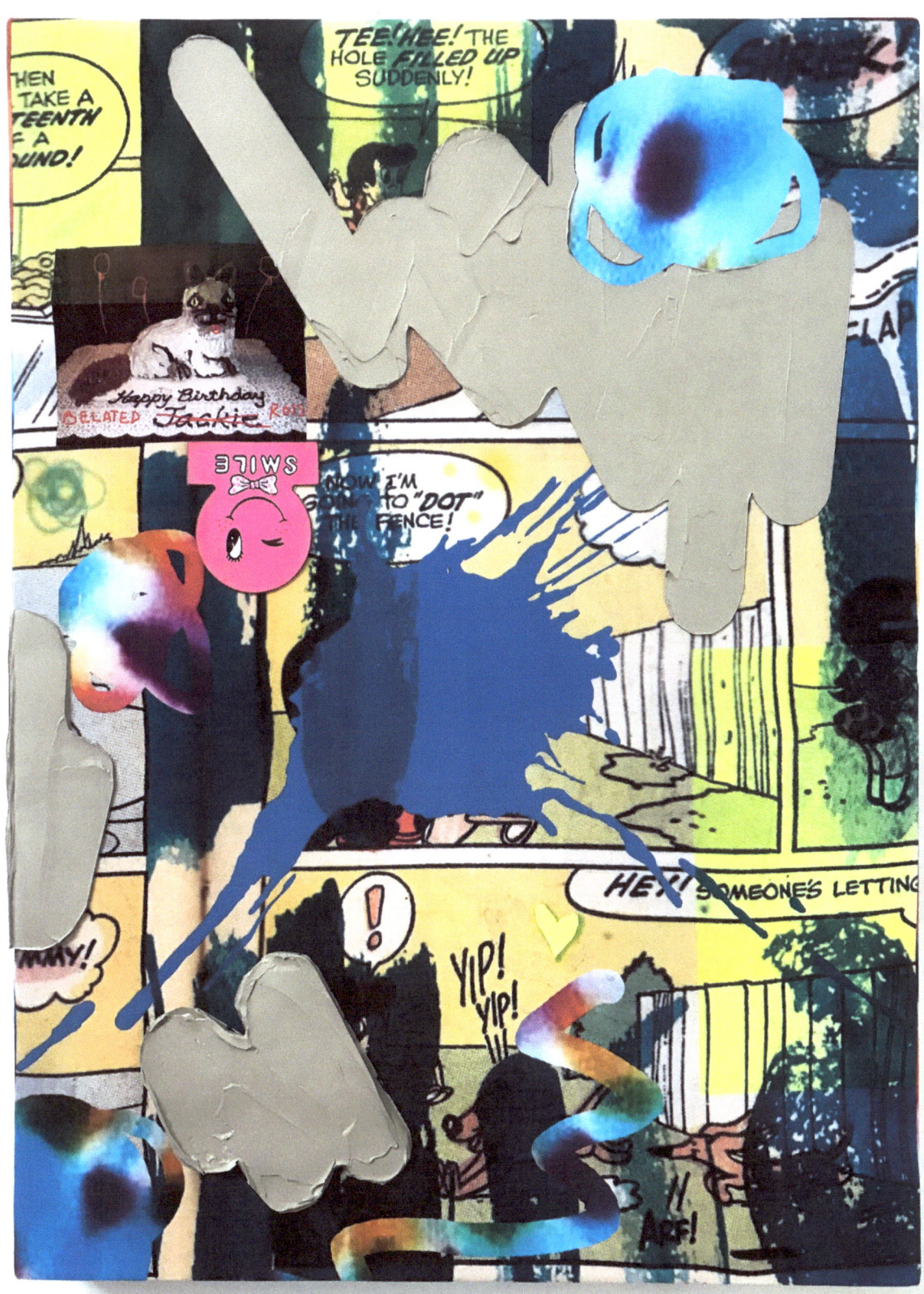

The images I cultivate often have origins in the realm of highly reproducible kitsch; the types of images bought from Target, Ikea, or Hobby Lobby and hung on the wall the same day. I seek to complicate the divide between these "outsider" cultures and contemporary art, not as a point of critique on either, but rather to create a relatable access point for all viewers. At the same time, I see the subjects and references associated with these "low-brow" art forms as reflections on current modes of visual communication in mainstream culture.

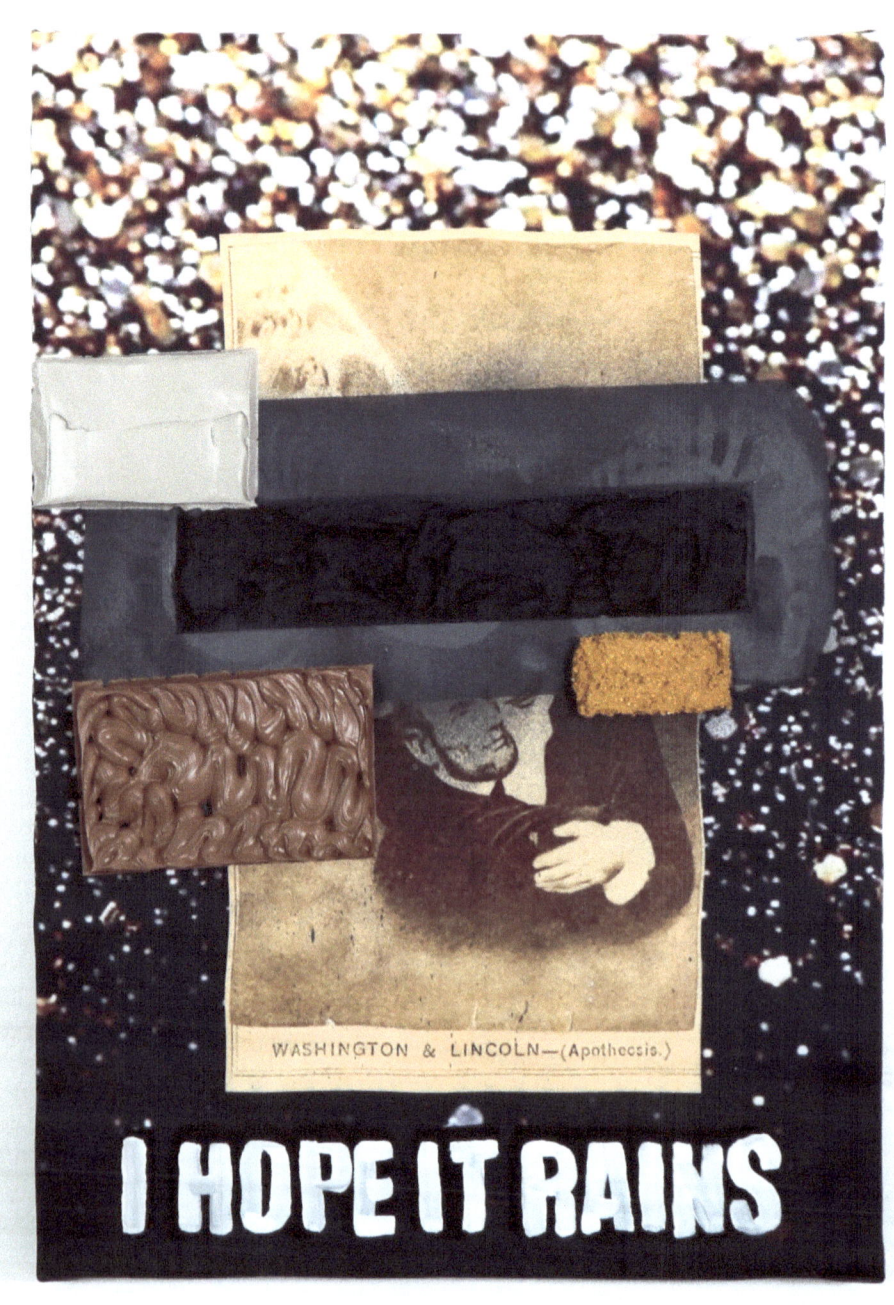

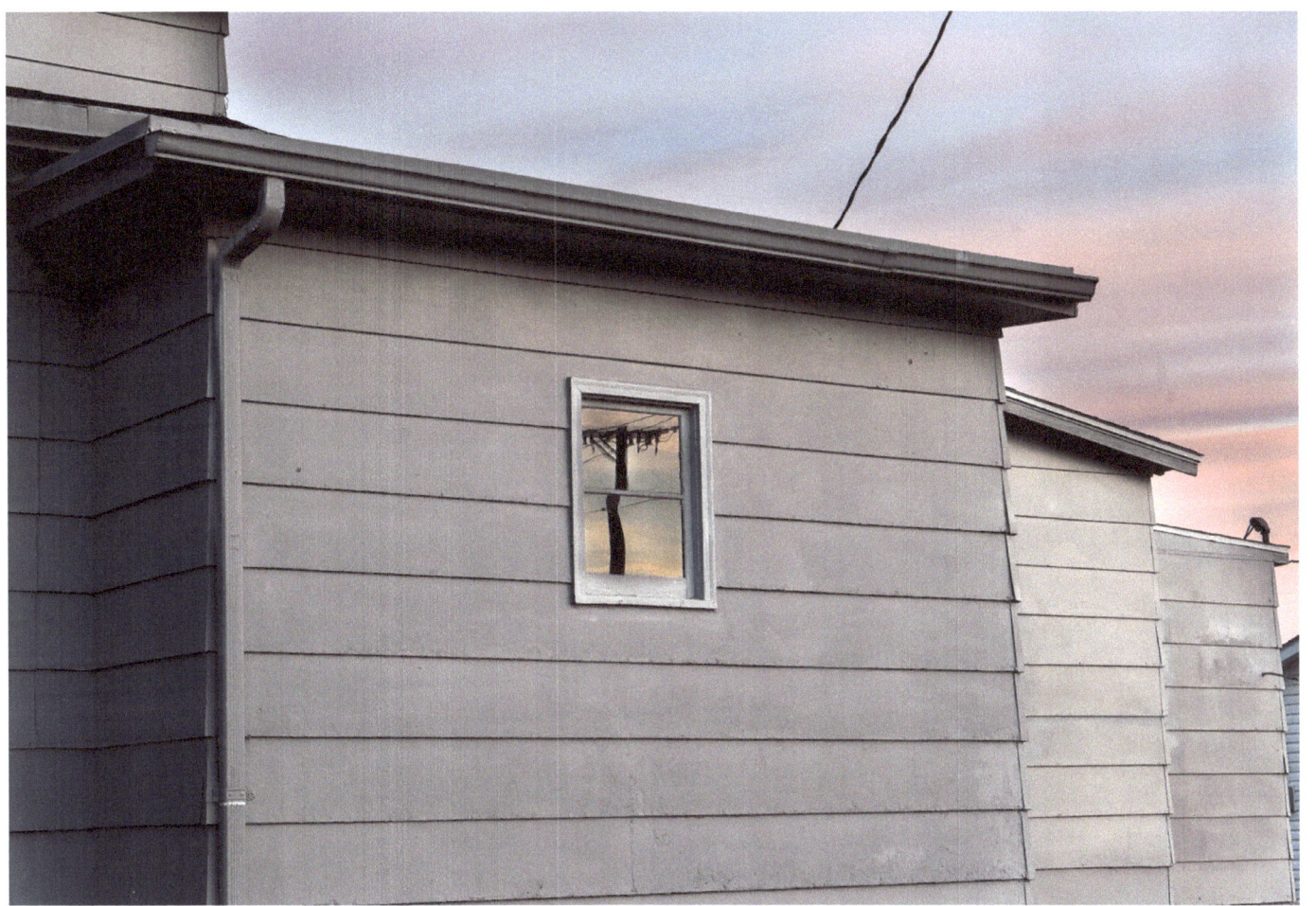

DEATH AND DESPAIR

A review of a photographic series by **Amanda Kaminski** Written by David Downs

It's about 8 pm and I've traveled from uptown via the red el train to the end of the orange to an empty street with a looming highway over pass above my head awash in the sound of rubber tires zooming across pavement. The air is warm and dry and it's the end of spring. The streets are familiar, though I always forget I've been here until I exit the train station. Down a narrow sidewalk, I traverse a puddle, balancing on planks of wood conveniently left in the right place acting as a shabby bridge across the water. There are old factories everywhere with Chinese pictographs and images showing food or restaurant supplies. If you can image Chelsea, NY or Chicago's West Loop before the galleries moved in... well before they were eaten alive by the boutiques and posh restaurants. This industrial corridor is still far enough removed to remain hidden away in a slumber for a bit longer.

There's art hiding away here at the address of 2727 S Mary Street in an unmarked building tucked away on a short curved road that's more of a driveway. It's a working space for several art studios in a warehouse and they regularly present shows of other artists in the gallery space between the studios. It's one of those refreshing spaces, lacking pretension. You're not always sure what kind of art you'll find here, but it's always worth taking a look.

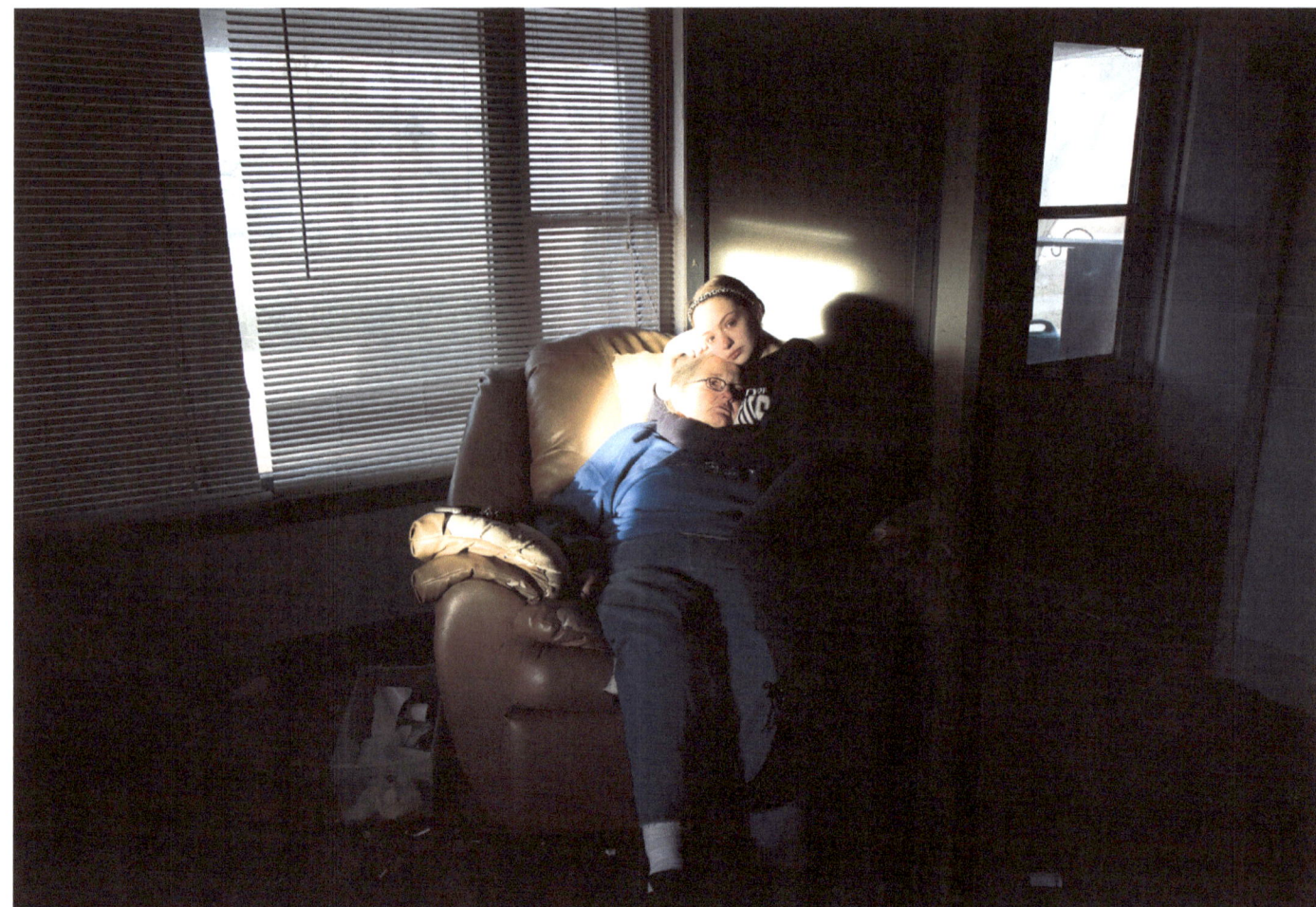

I came here to see the new work of photographer, Amanda Kaminski. I had known her from earlier work dealing with body issues and coming-of-age into womanhood. What surprised me in this new series titled, "Death and Despair" is the lack of confrontational imagery. Instead of dramas, these images speak in a softer tone, almost a whisper, of sadness, strength, and triumph of the spirit. In a sentimental, yet documentarian style, Kaminski shares the story of her aging mother after the loss of her partner of 20 years, as well as having to sell the house Amanda grew up in. It's a touching series that took the artist two years to finally realize due to the emotional content.

The acceptance of the sentimental in Amanda's work is what really gives this series strength beyond the technical skill of the photographer. A true caring for the subject matter prevails over camera positioning, composition, and lighting. I stress this, as it is proven here in Amanda's photographs that photography can portray sentiment honestly and openly in opposition to most other forms of modern visual art which have long since shunned sentiment. We see the story in the still frames cinematically and then insert ourselves in the images or replace the figures with ones from our own memories until the photographs become like snapshots of our own experiences. The photographer is afforded a certain anonymity and can be easily replaced by the viewer who takes possession of the image as a remembered or imagined circumstance of their own.

https://www.amandakaminski.com

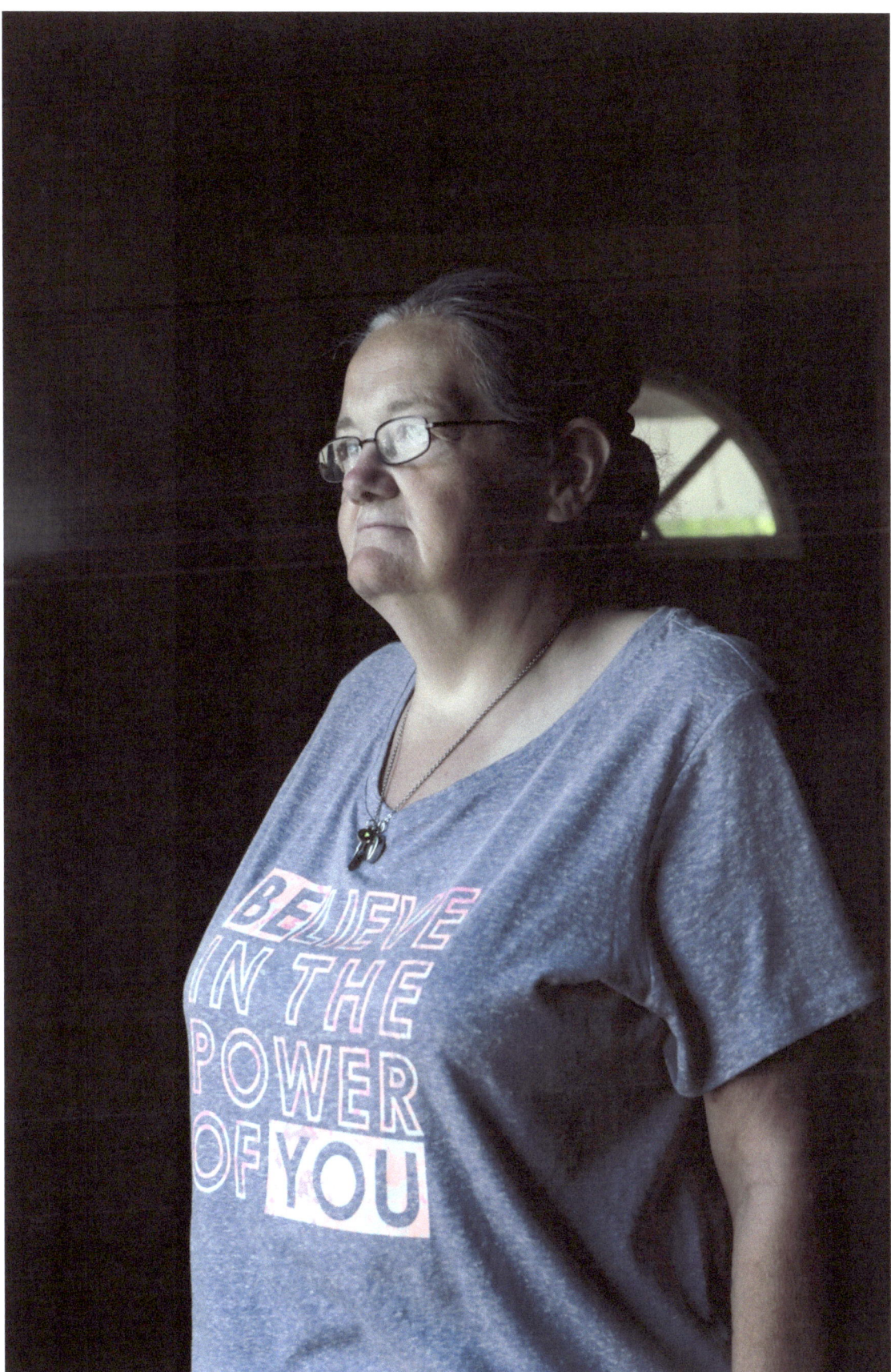

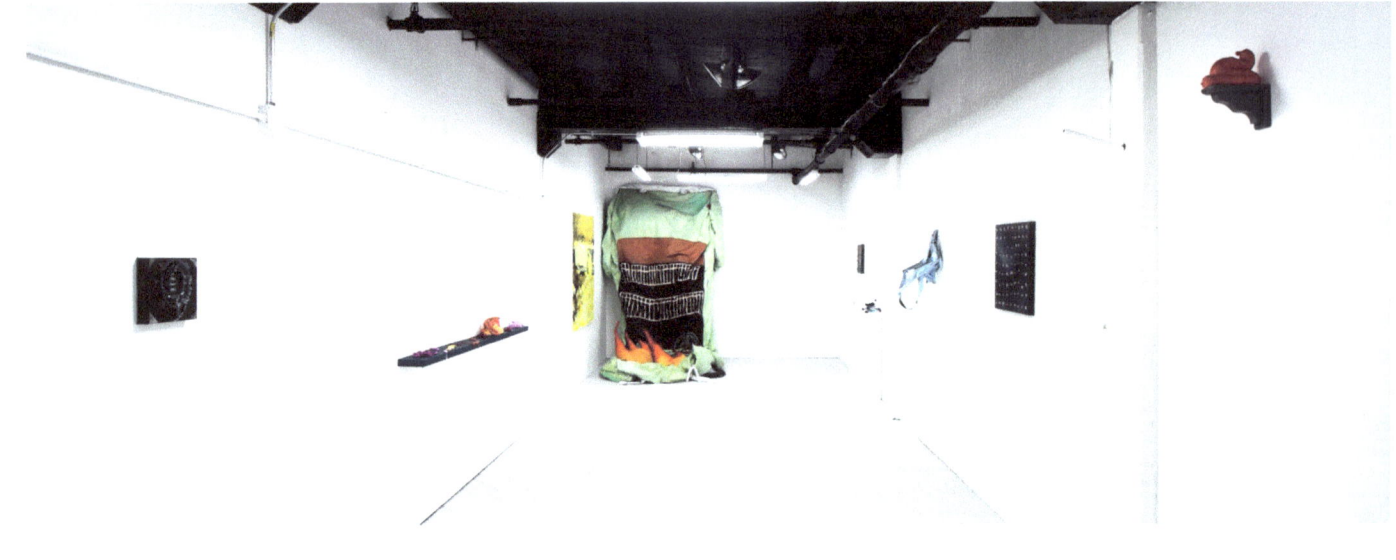

MATERIAL OBJECTIVITY

Baby Blue Gallery · 2201 S. Halsted, Chicago, IL 60608

January 11 · February 2, 2019

Artists Cindy Bernhard, David Downs, Boris Ostrerov, and Erin Smego explore varied ways of expanded painting. By transgressing a painting's conventional parameters of the flat rectangular surface, the artists use paint not to create illusion, but to bring the material into the space of the viewer. Each apply paint or fabric to materials long used in creating painting surfaces (stretchers/panels) albeit in an innovative way – making paint rest on flat substrates, protrude from the surface material, and use unconventional shapes as supports. While engaging in several forms of mark making, tactility, and physical depth, each artist's work explores individual themes and ideas with their materials as they reference historical traditions and social constructs. In an age where much of art viewing is seen through compressed jpegs, these 'painted sculptures' yearn for adequate embodied viewing which only an exhibition space can provide.

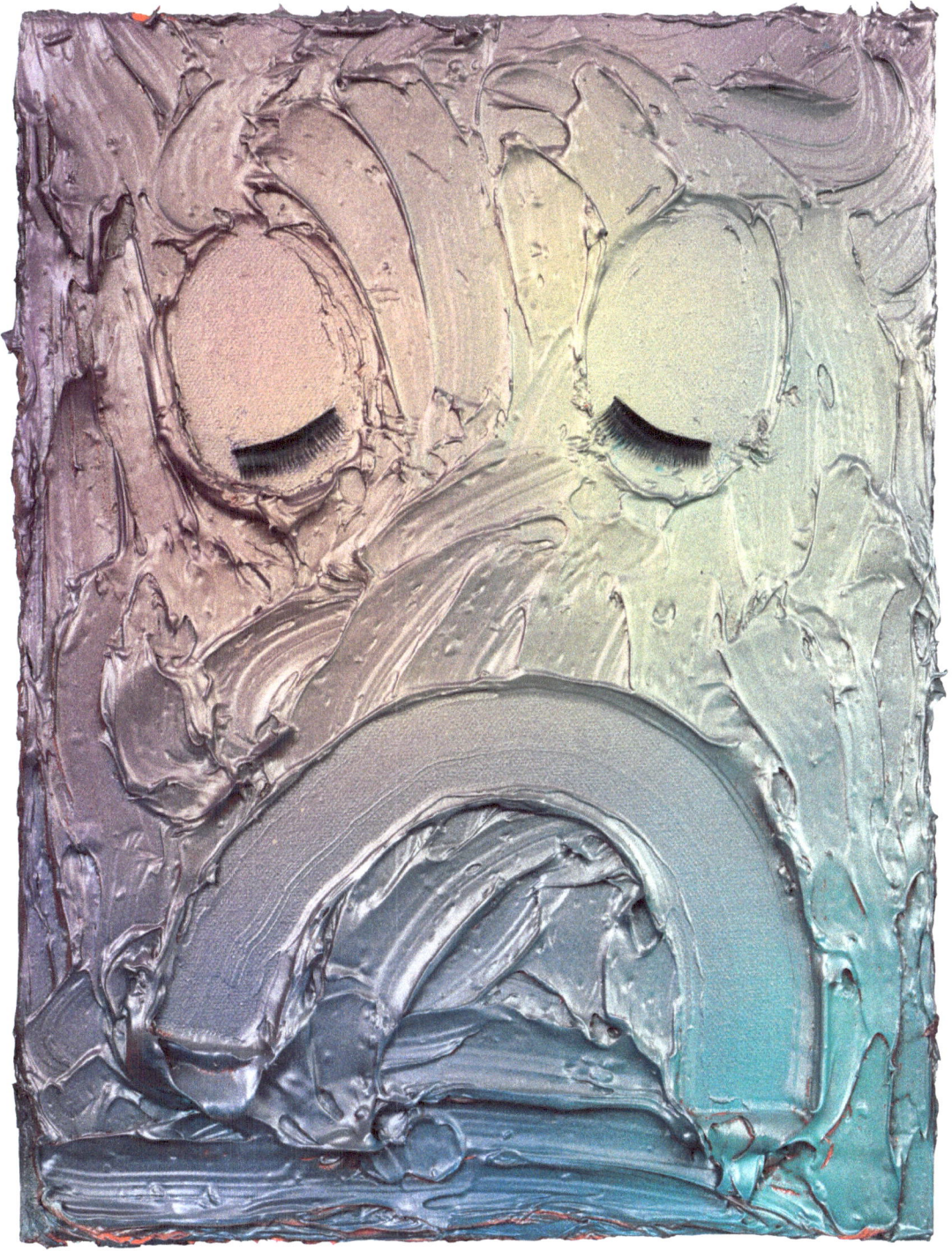

Image on this page: Cindy Bernhard
Previous page: installation view

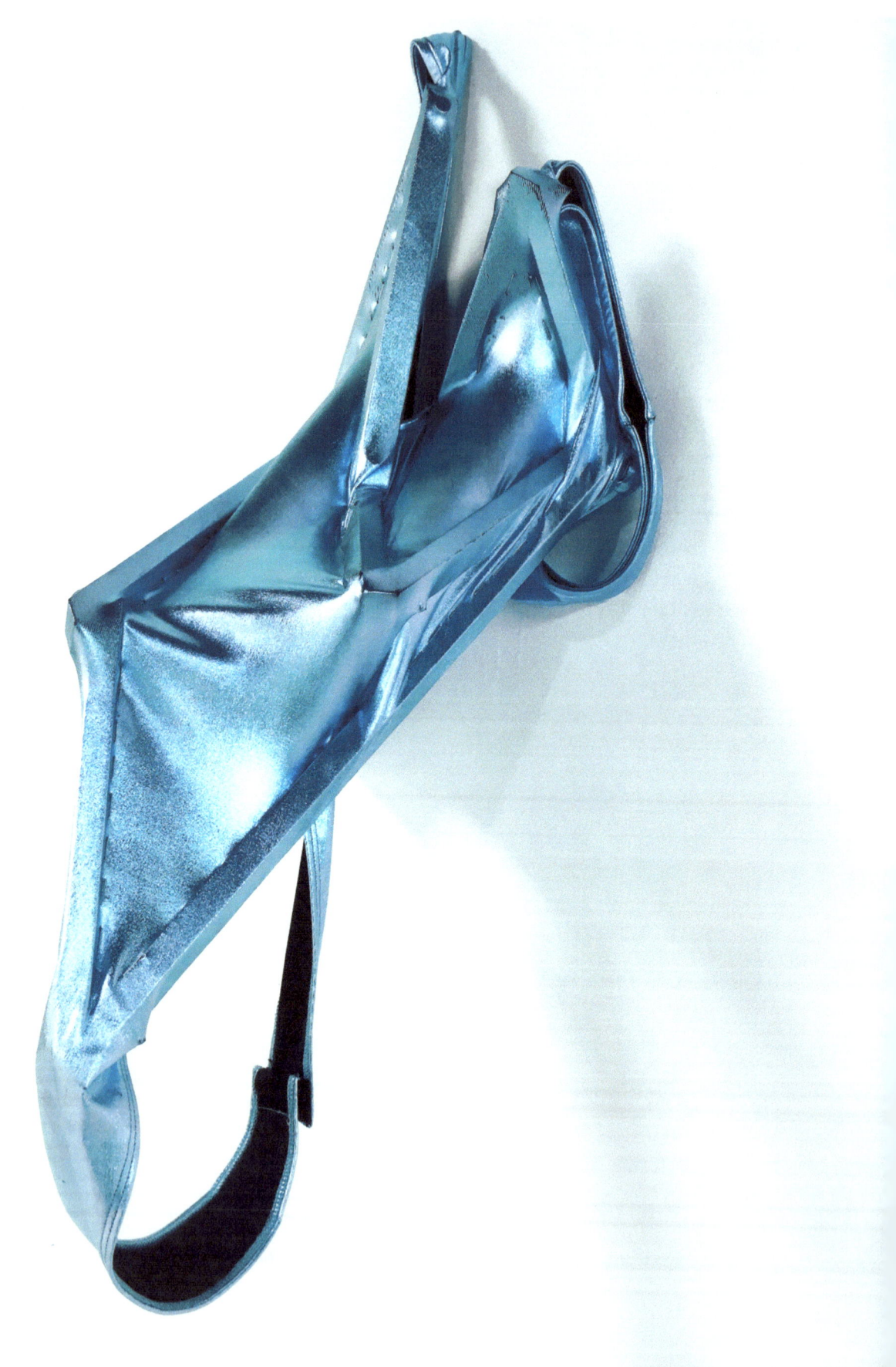

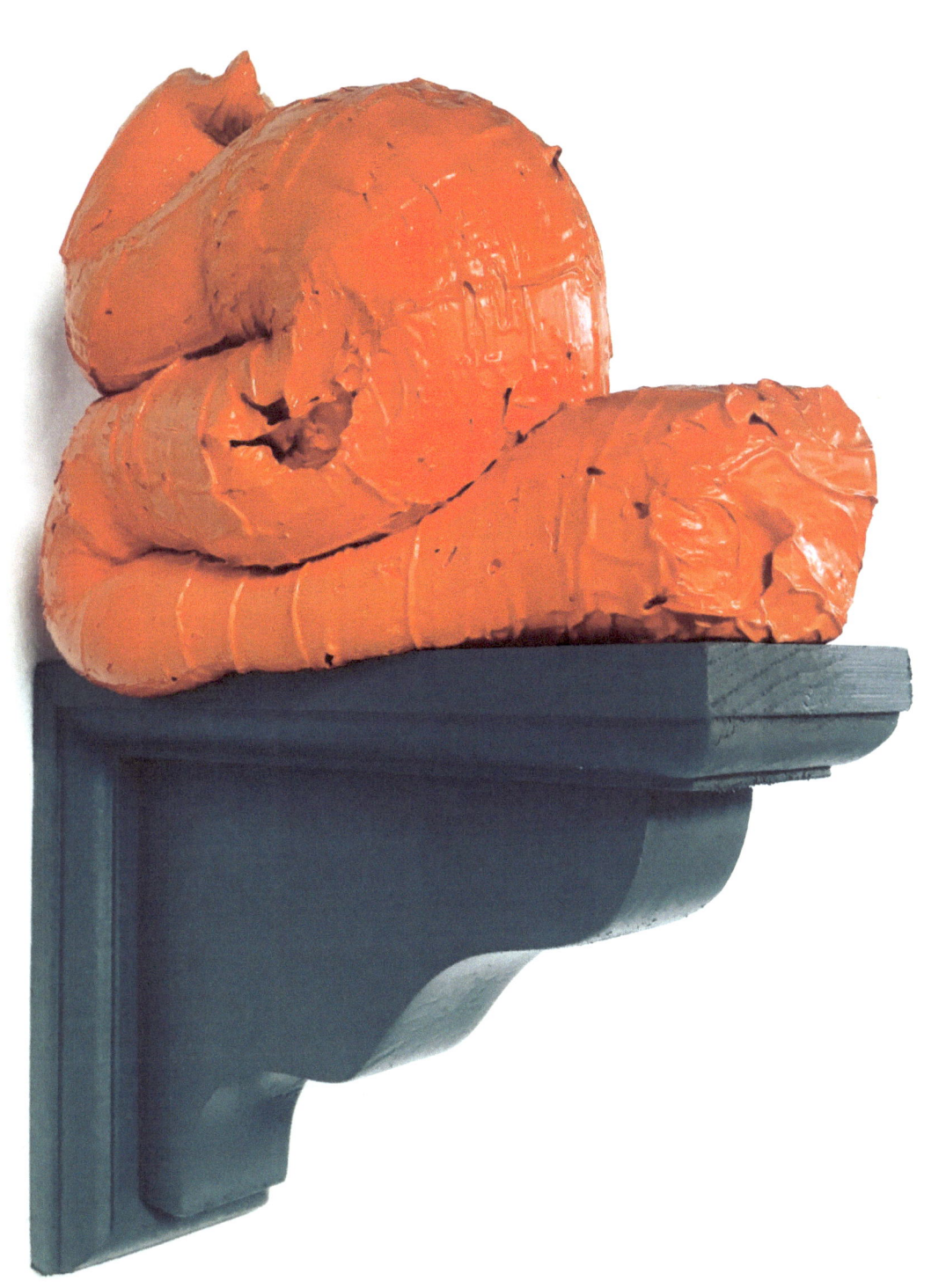

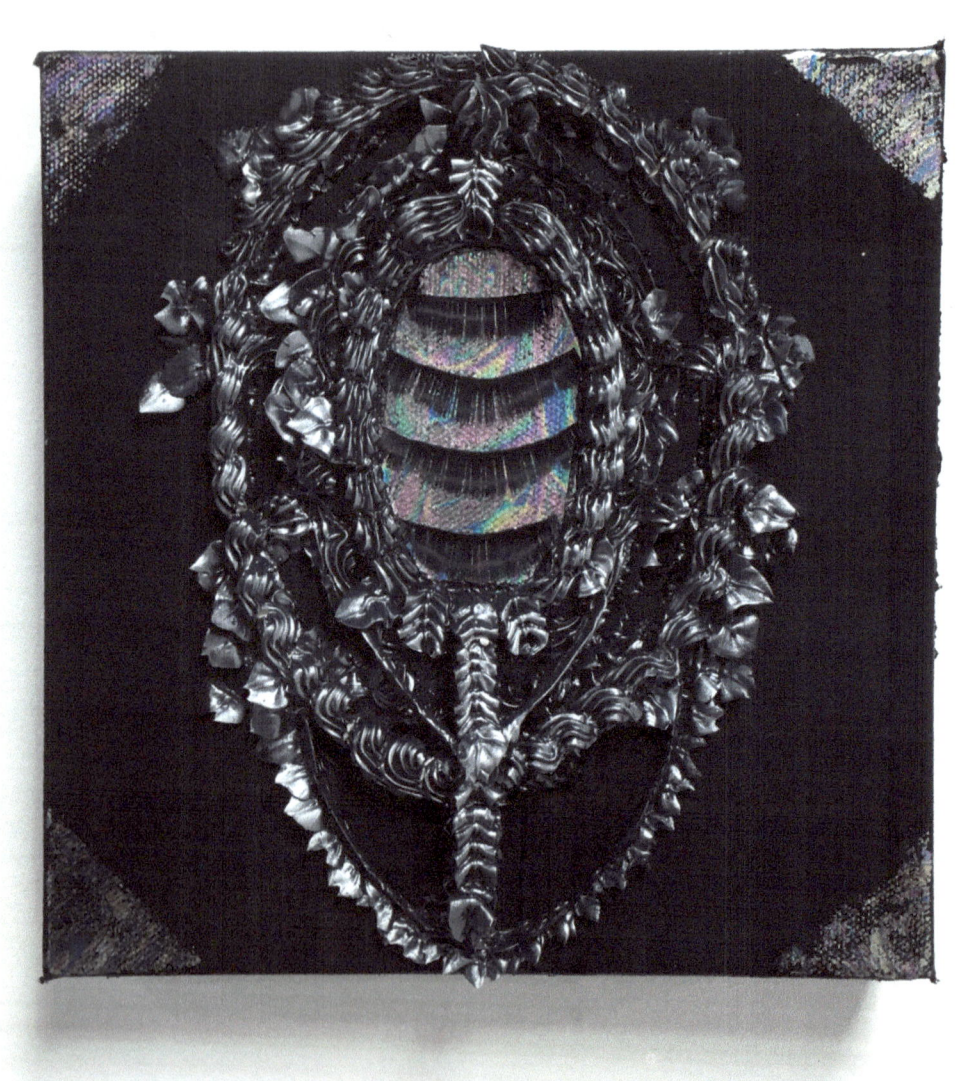

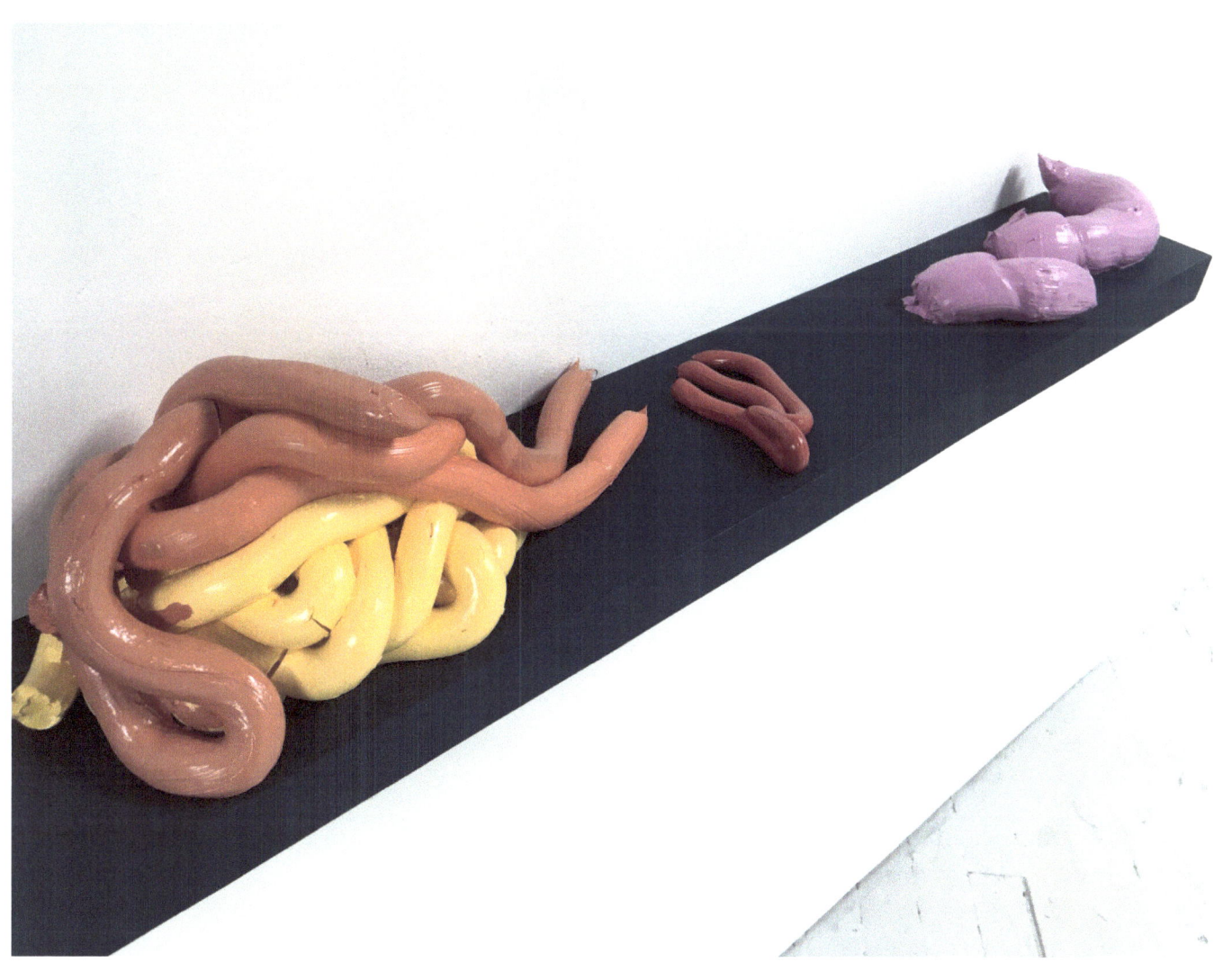

Previous pages: Erin Smego, Boris Ostrerov, Cindy Bernhard
This page: Boris Ostrerov

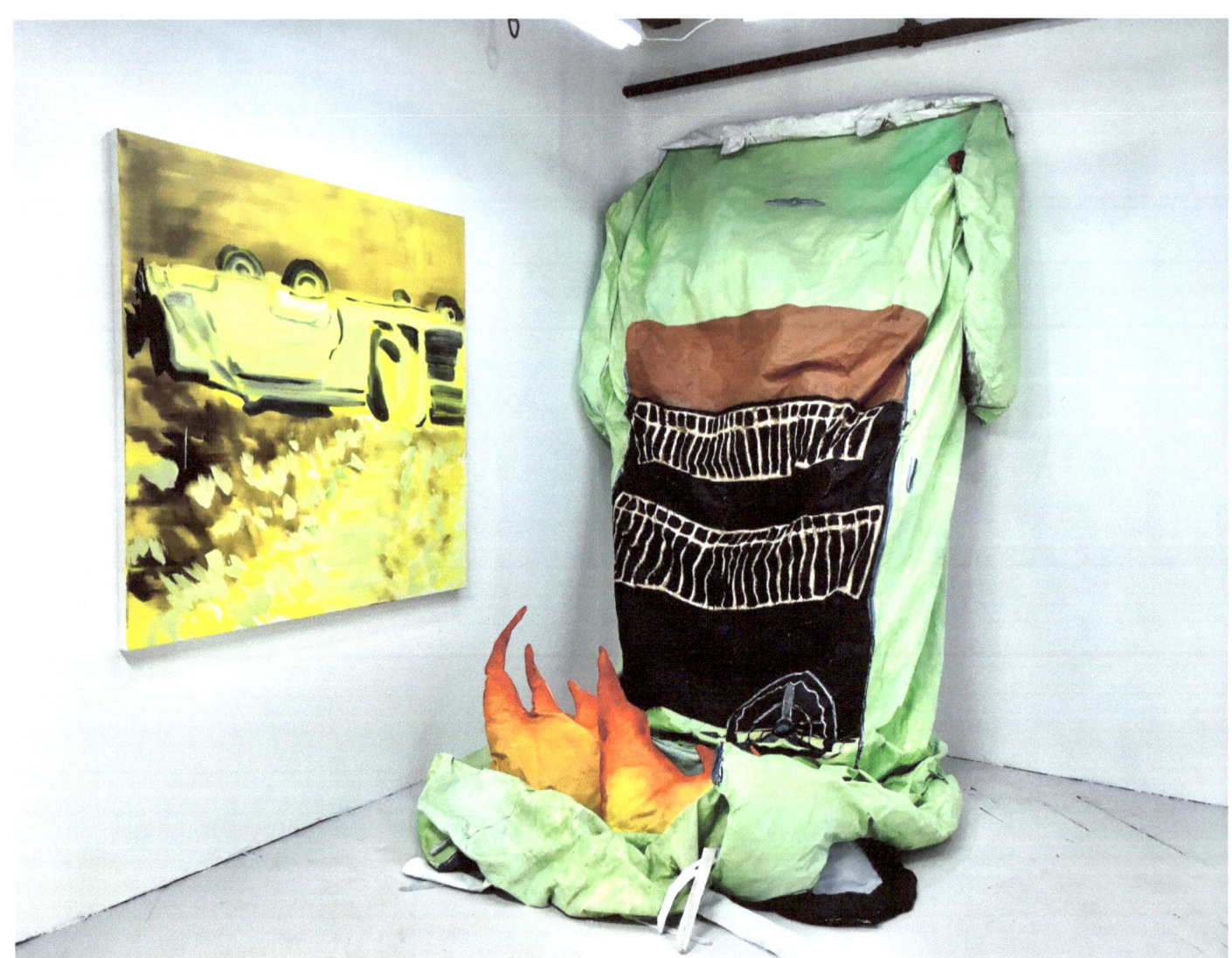

This page: David Downs
Next page: Erin Smego

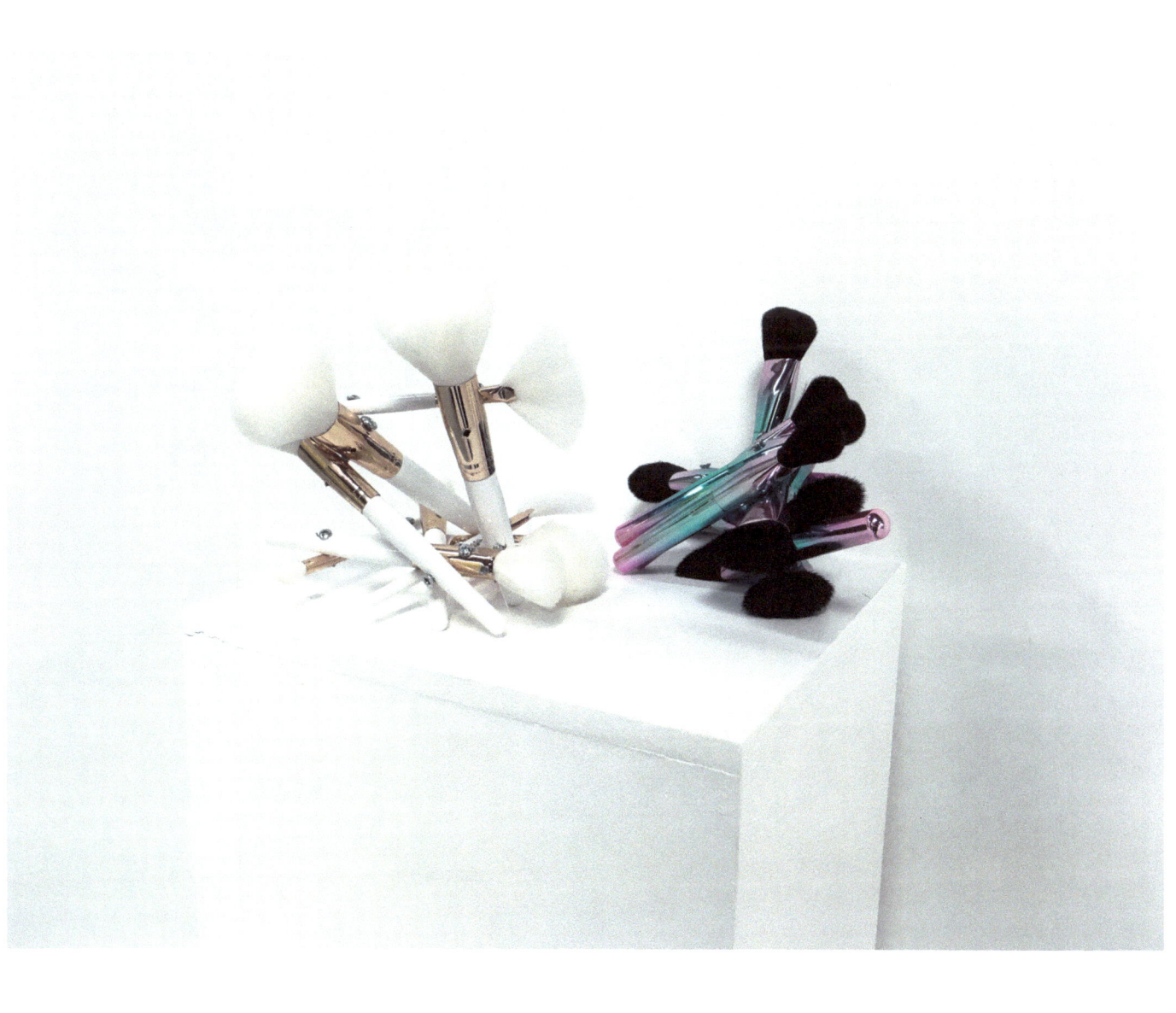

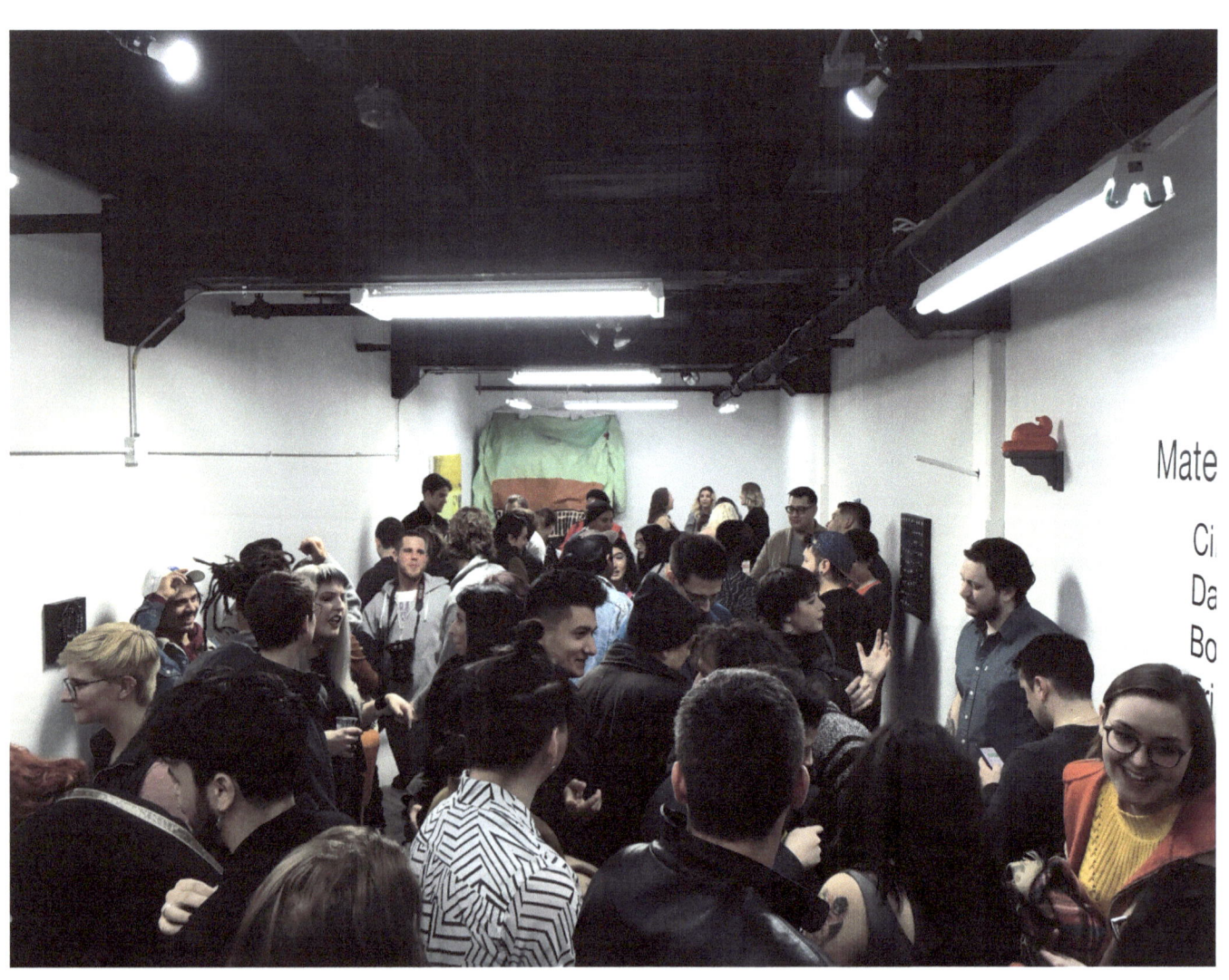

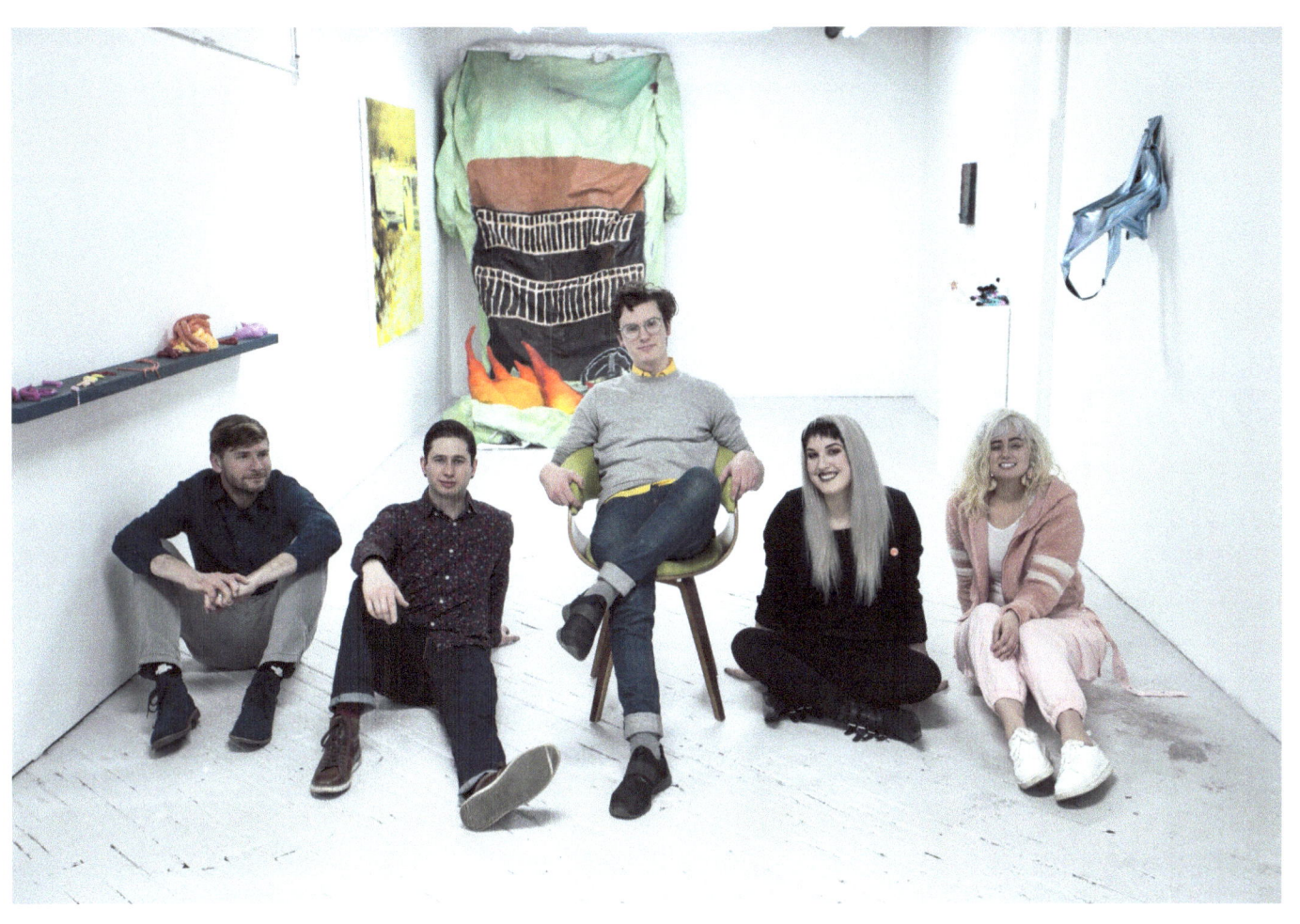

(From left) David Downs, Boris Ostrerov, Caleb Beck (owner of Baby Blue Gallery), Cindy Bernhard, and Erin Smego

ABSTRACT NOW

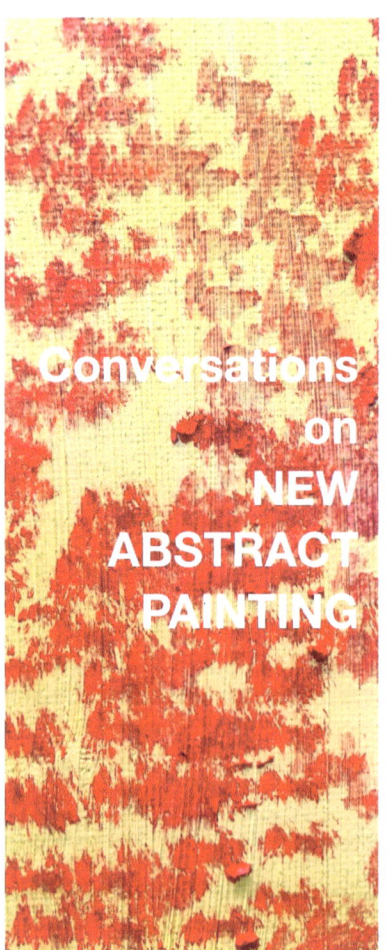

Conversations on NEW ABSTRACT PAINTING

It's 1949 in East Village, New York City. Willem de Kooning scrapes away a juicy slip of oil paint with his palette knife and it lands on the floor in a heap. With a large brush he slathers the cleared area with another fatty layer of oil paint. He gives and he takes from the canvas, alternating between brush and knife. He drinks liquor straight from the bottle and wipes the sweat from his brow beneath a wild frock of platinum hair. He hasn't forgotten the fight with his friend, that gruff bastard, Jackson Pollock, at The Club earlier. He narrowly missed being struck in the head by the bathroom door Jackson had ripped from its hinges and flung at him. The feelings are added to a building new anxiety and a need to prove himself to himself on the surface of a large foreboding canvas...

It's all very romantic in retrospect; the camaraderie, the competition, the poverty, the suffering, and the triumphs against the odds. It reminds us of a different time when a small group of dedicated artists could take the art world from Paris and bring it home to the US and especially to New York City. This was the time of the "Abstract Expressionists" or the "New York School" where macho men (and a few macho women) fought for a new and unique American style of painting. They met in cafes to drink cheap coffee and argue their points with the intellect of philosophers but the sophistication of cowboys. Of course, as all movements do, this one was eventually superseded by the next; the stark control of minimalism, the sheen of pop, the grit of neoexpressionism, etc. In the minds of a lot of painters, however, my self included, we are still competing with the giants of then. How do our ideas and techniques measure up? Just where is our Cedar or Club? Are we lost to nostalgia or is there something new and exciting still to be discovered in abstraction?

At the end of 2014 I publish the second book in the "Polonium" series titled, Nonobject. I featured various artists creating work that I thought would fit the idea of non-objective abstraction. I too was experimenting with abstract painting with a desire to understand abstraction more intimately. By this time I could paint just about anything representationally. It was the idea of inventing something out of myself that was more appealing and challenging at the time. I found that when I went to museums and art galleries I spent most of my time looking at the abstract work. I wanted to see the invention of shapes and strokes as well as the textures. Obviously there was a lot more to it than that but I was still learning. Among my peers, I discovered many abstract painters that really knew their stuff. They weren't rehashing an old style, they were inventing and reinventing. I was curious if they still questioned, as I did, their place and contribution to the history of abstract painting. I created a small list of questions in an effort to arouse a new conversation about their work. I've included a few of those responses here in this article.

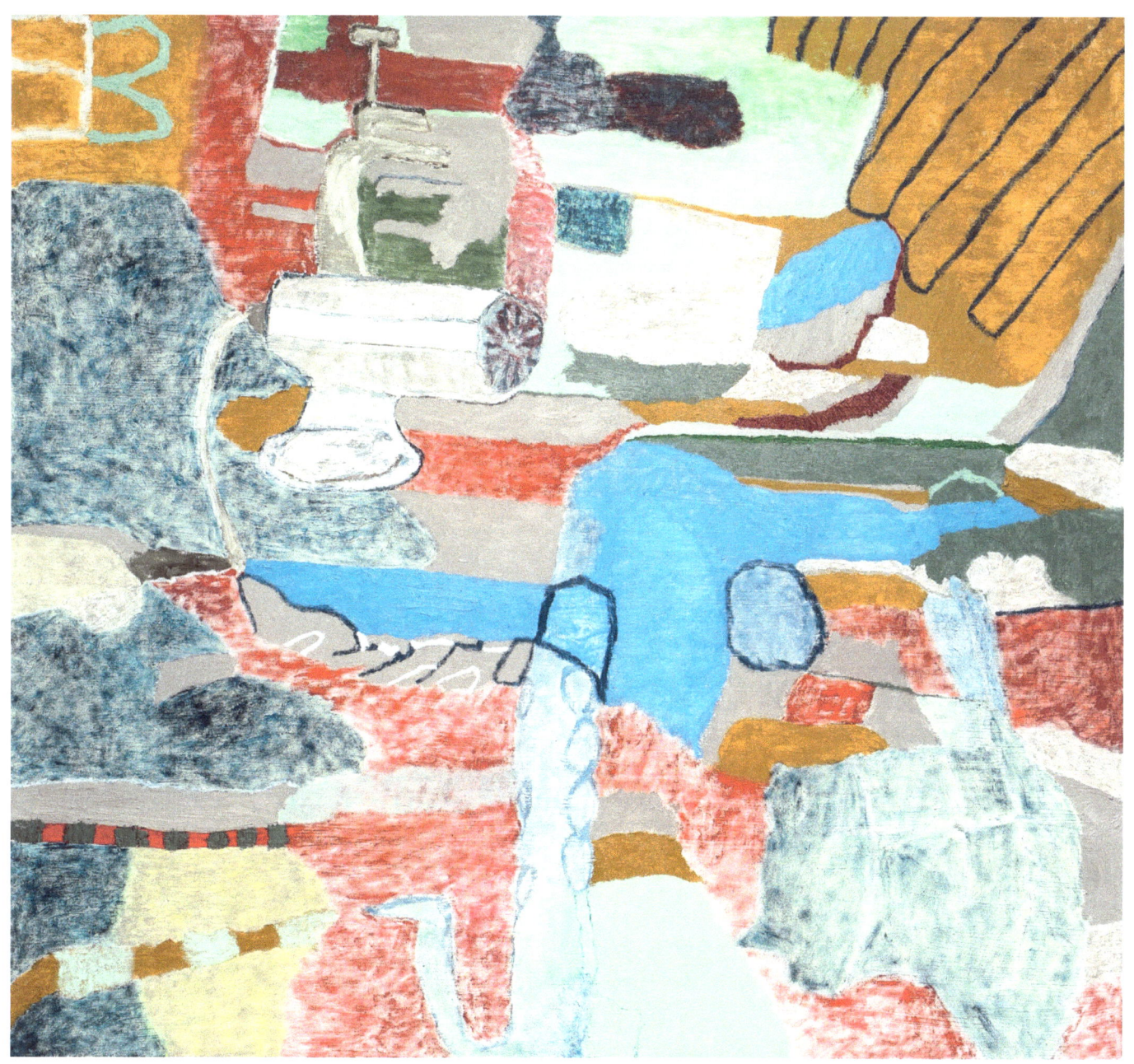

Jeffrey Sanderson

Do you identify as an abstract painter? Is that distinction important to you?

I identify with the term, and I do consider myself to be an abstract painter, but I also quibble with and question it. When I am working on a painting myself, descriptive and categorical distinctions about the work are not in my mind.

On the other hand, when I'm out in the world and looking at art in general, distinctions between abstract and representational art sometimes come up for me. Stories and interpretations, along with my awareness of art history creeps into my mind, so works that are non-objective can feel quite different than objective ones.

The many modes of expression available are all valid, and some of my favorite paintings are by folks who paint in objective, symbolic, representational modes.

What ideas are you exploring through abstract painting?

I supposed one question I find myself digesting constantly is a question Guston framed as (approximately!) 'what goes where?' What marks, made with my brush, with paint that can be thick or thin, drippy or solid, in colors or neutral, scumbled or solid, and so forth, onto the 'where' that is space within my canvas. Plus, proportions, weights, amounts, and the balance of the marks affects me and is a primary

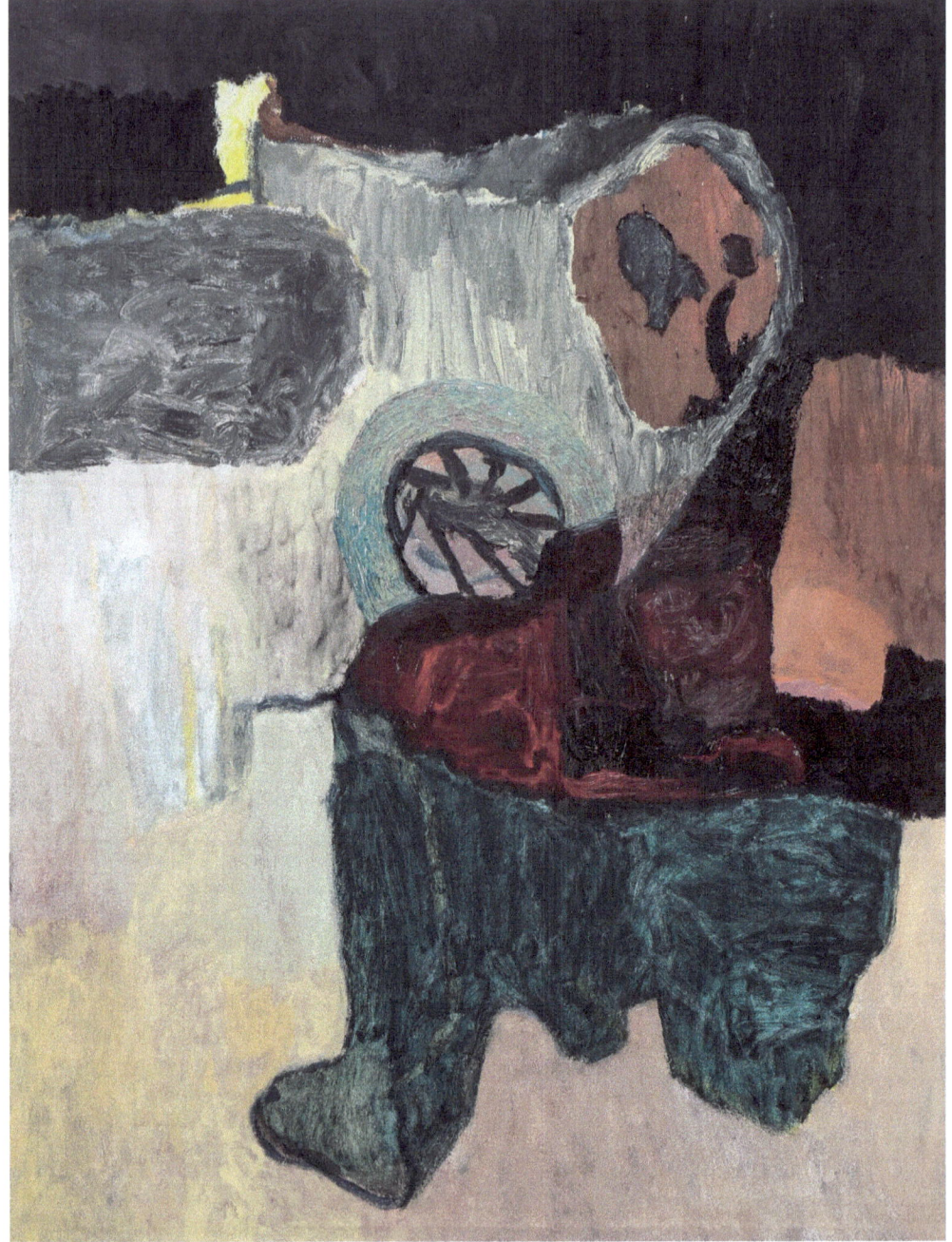

consideration for me in the moments when I'm making the work. Relationships, how one thing affects another, and all sorts of traditional 'painterly' questions are the things I find myself questioning and working through.

How are you referencing the history of abstract painting, or challenging it, or does that even matter?

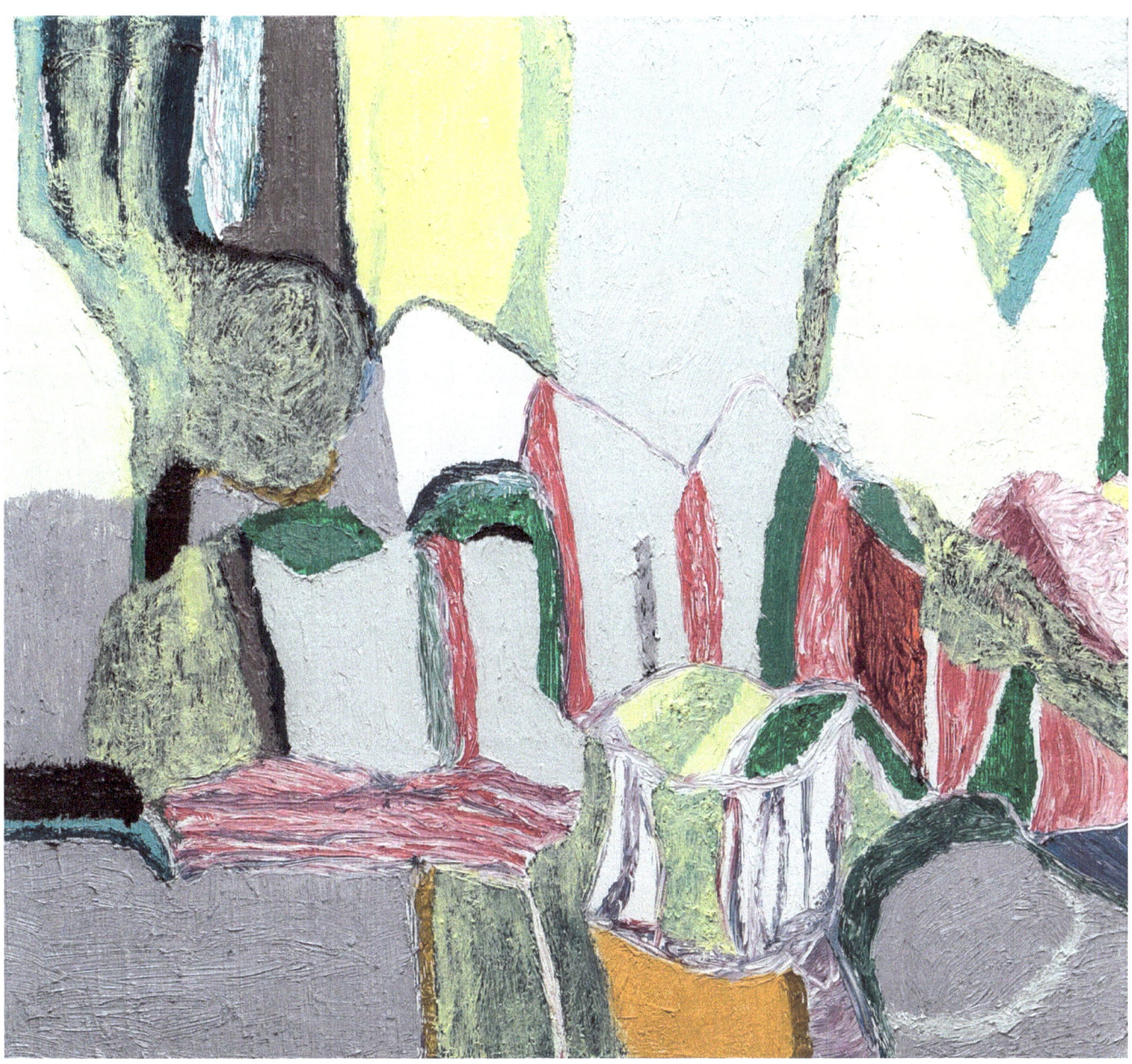

I'm grateful to painters and artists who have created works that move and interest me. But I'm not really thinking about challenging, venerating, or addressing history while I'm in the studio. In a sense, I feel like a builder who has a need for very specific tools or instruments, so painting for me is perhaps all about finding and using the tools I've realized I need.

The history of painting and art-making more broadly has tuned my senses, so what matters as I turn inwards to my own work and process is the reactions I have to my creative 'circumstances'. The reactions are formed into choices that I make in my own works.

Is the materiality of paint or the action of painting important to your work? Could the work be made in any other medium?

Yes, the material is quite important to me and paint is essential to my work. I find myself rather addicted to manipulating paint and other materials. Paint is special to me, and oil paint is clearly a magical substance! I care about paint, probably more than anyone should. While I do also make art out of assembled objects, and I draw and sometimes make photographs, I consider myself a painter and the works made with paint are dependent on the whims of this engaging and ineffable substance.

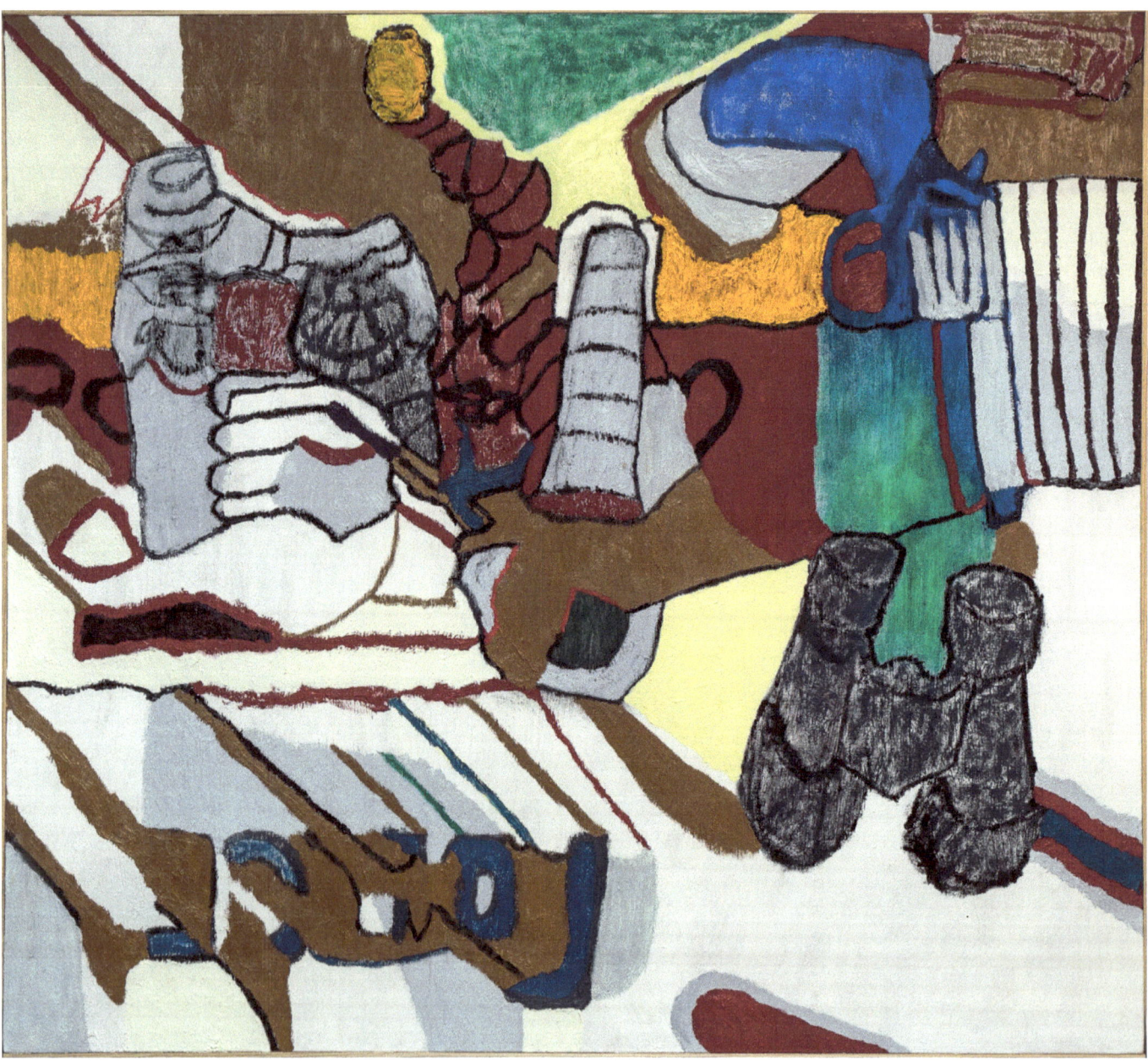

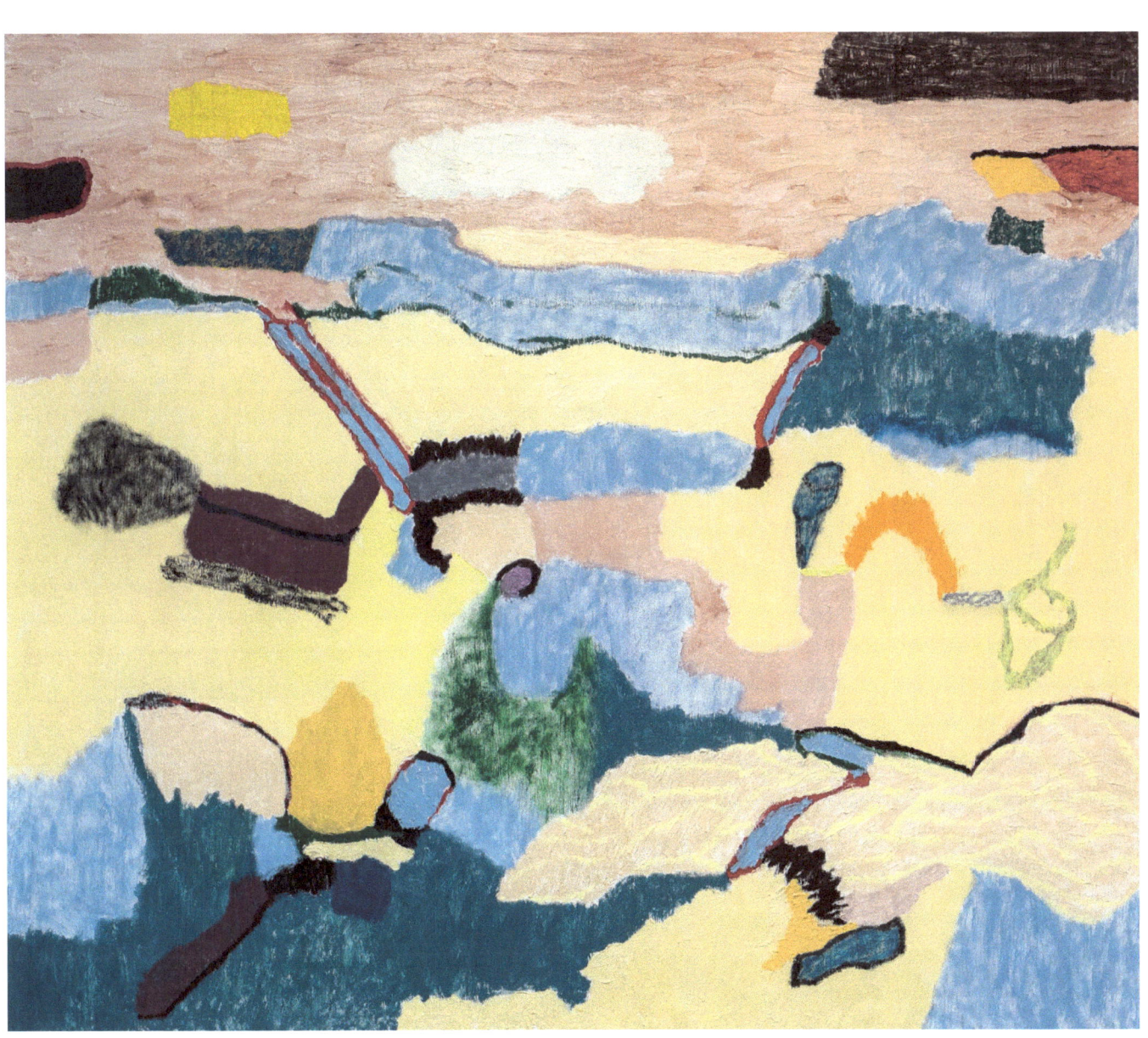

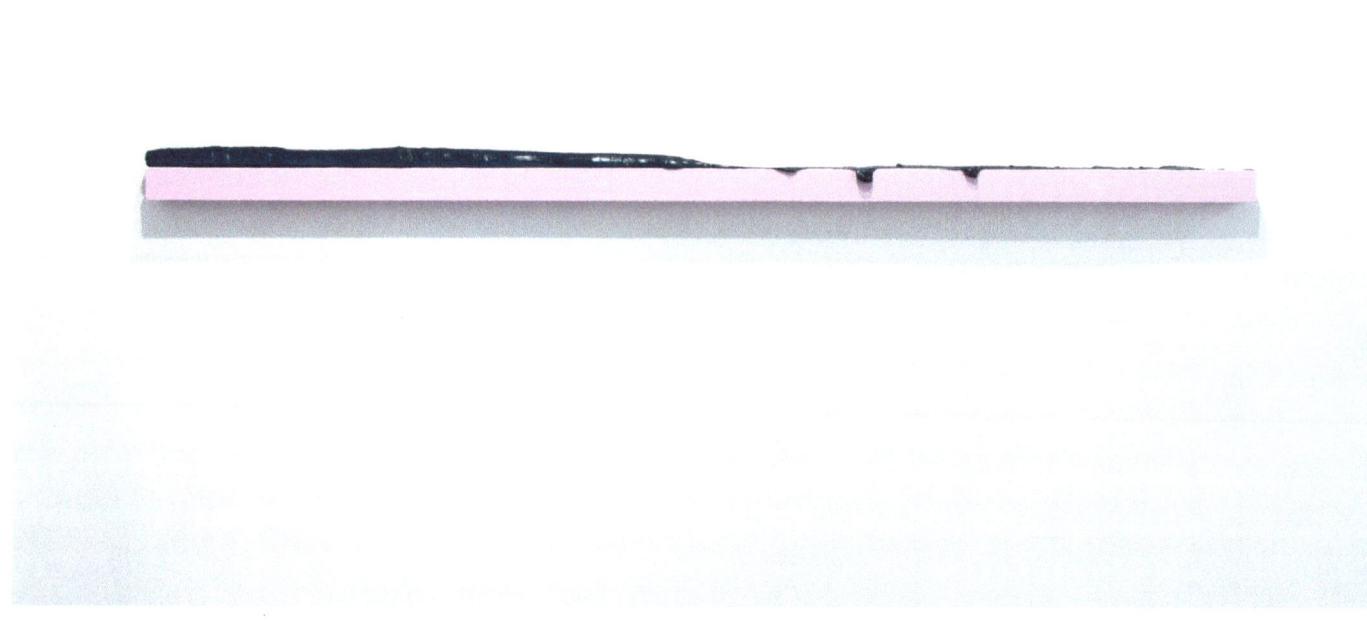

Boris Ostrerov

Do you identify as an abstract painter? Is that distinction important to you?

My work appears abstract but i wouldn't rush to put it in the abstract camp; it is what it is. I'm putting paint on display though i'm aware that the squeezes and support have references and resemble things other than themselves.

What ideas are you exploring through abstract painting?

In general I'm exploring play, excretions, extremes, gestures, actions, narrative, and commodity.

How are you referencing the history of abstract painting, or challenging it, or does that even matter?

Do you mean pure abstract painting?

I am like scraping up all the paint off of the surface of the paintings, (imagine that the paint is wet) separating the different colors, and squeezing it back out of a tube-like opening. Sometimes in neatly organized piles, other times in more aggressive gestures. These piles which can look like shit poke fun of traditional paintings as they downgrade the canvas to the function of a literal "support." And they declare that all paintings, like Pollock, Mondrian, Joan Mitchell, etc., even representational ones that are windows to other world, are just paint on canvas. I find that humorous ;).

I also enjoy proposing looking at paintings not perpendicular to the face of them, but from the side as if all the bumps of paint and texture were exaggerated heavily. People can walk across my paintings and around them. I'm currently working on a few pieces that are to be

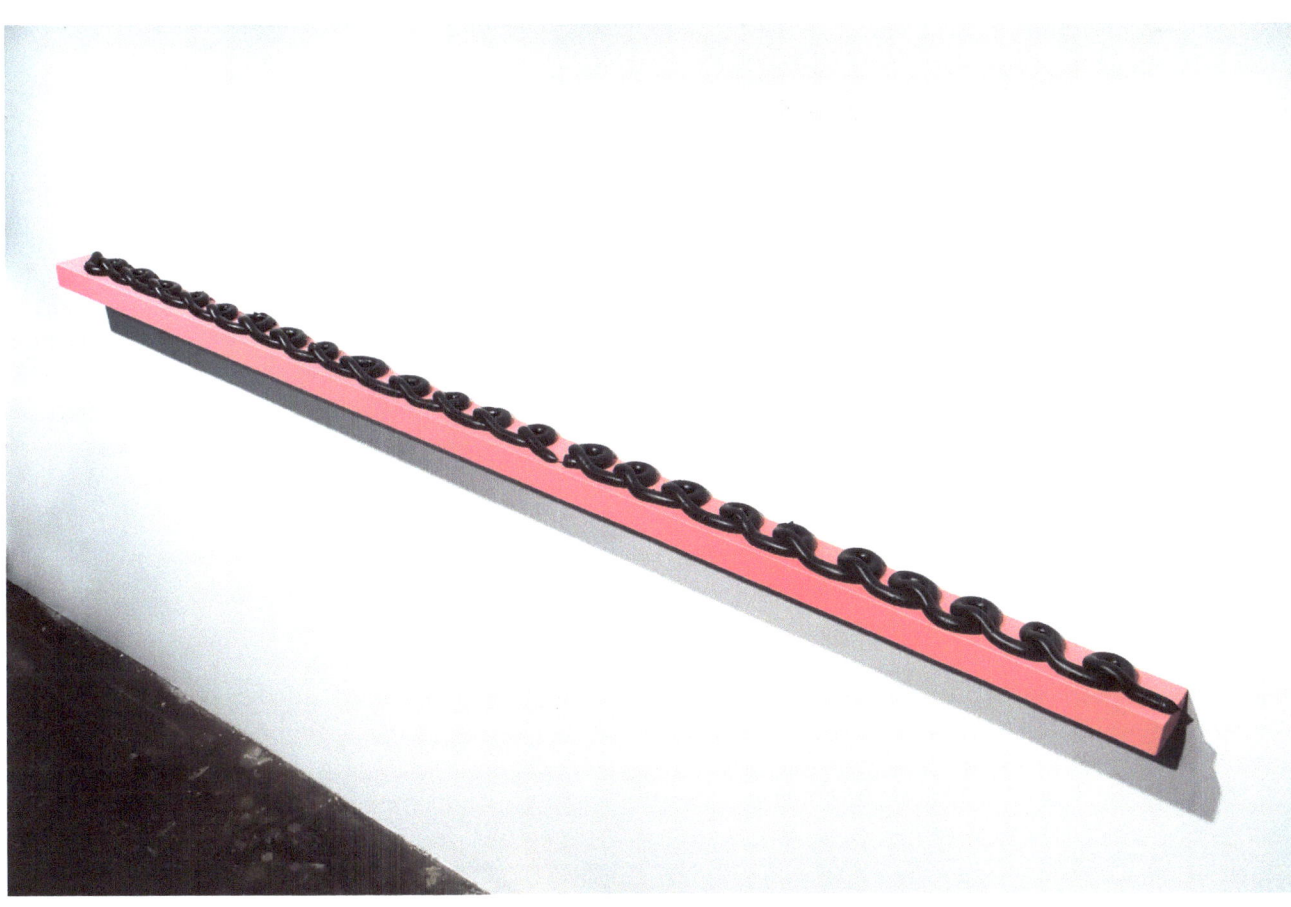

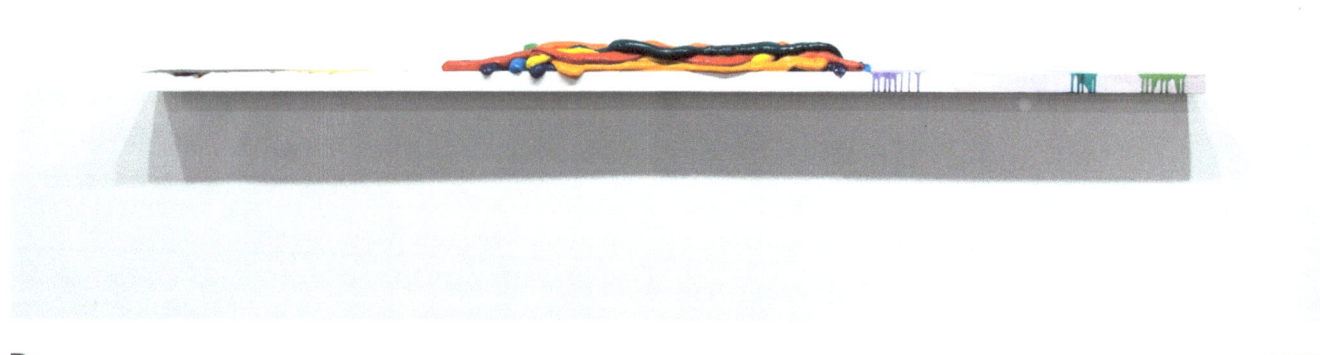

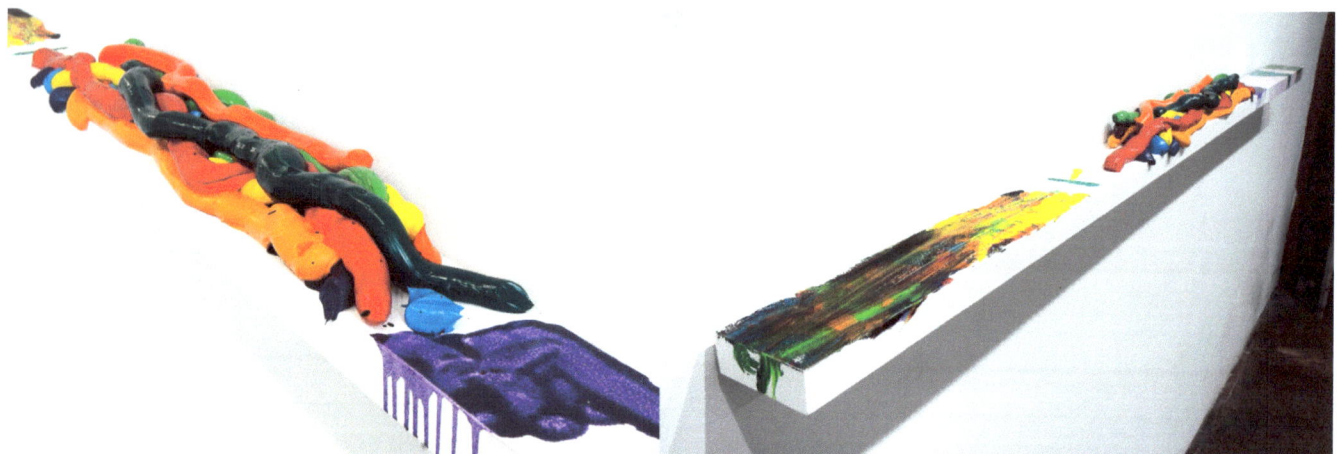

shown laying flat on their back on a pedestal and viewers can see them from a near birds-eye perspective. That challenges how people think of abstract painting.

Is the materiality of paint or the action of painting important to your work? Could the work being made and any other medium?

Using acrylic is like having sex with a condom. You can't use anything but oil paint for my work because that would be faking it! It wouldn't be pushing the medium to it's extreme. I like pushing it to the extreme. Makes it surprising too! Acrylic...meh, it was designed to be used thinly and VERY thickly.

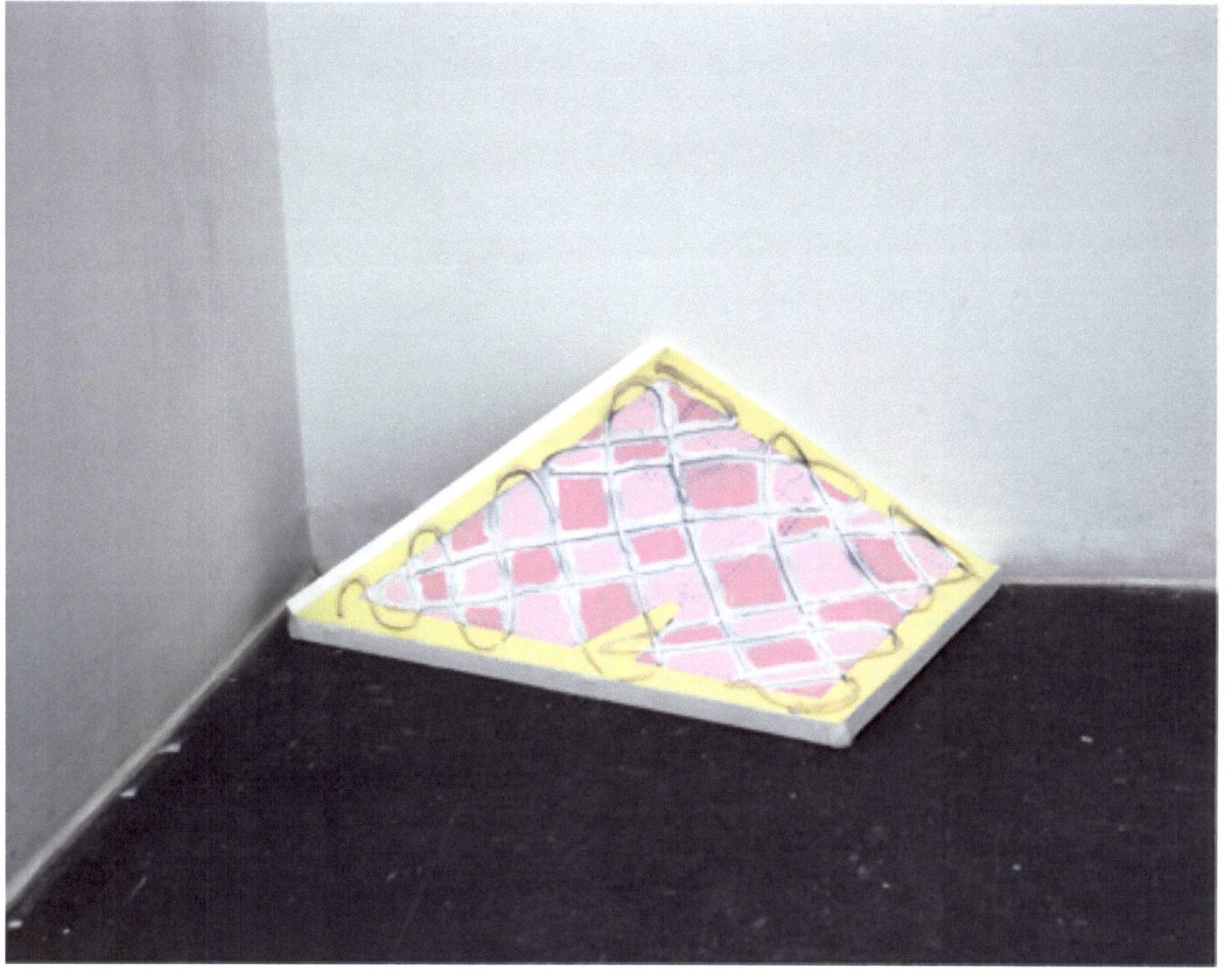

Caleb Beck

What ideas are you exploring through abstract painting?

In part I explore the silliness of the connection between looking and thinking. As humans we have these somewhat innate or at least intuitive assumptions and perceptions about the world, e.g., things have mass, up is up and down is down, object permanence etc. We aestheticize these in ways and create art that feels natural but whose structure is very unnatural. In laymen terms, art reformulates life through a human filter, it feels right to us but that filter is so wrong. For a long time painting functioned as a window, you looked into another space the *painting space*, modernism rejected the window and brought painting to the surface, now I think a lot of painters including myself are combining the two. Forcing painting to fluctuate between surface and window, figure-ground reversal is an amazing psychological effect. But to further my more general point, the conventions and artifice of painting reveal how we think, like following an MC Escher staircase until it loops perfectly back in on itself and we realize we've been duped. I think this is the cerebral side of my work, the very left brained and formalist side of my thinking. If a painting didn't get beyond this it'd be a cute prank on our psyche but nothing really more. The emotional and affective side of my paintings come from color and image. Color hits you in your gut and floods your reptile brain well before your able to process it into literal meaning. Image brings in metaphor and association, which adds a poetic element to painting. This juggling act if done right hits on some level that makes me feel more engaged and in love with life, as cheesy as that sounds

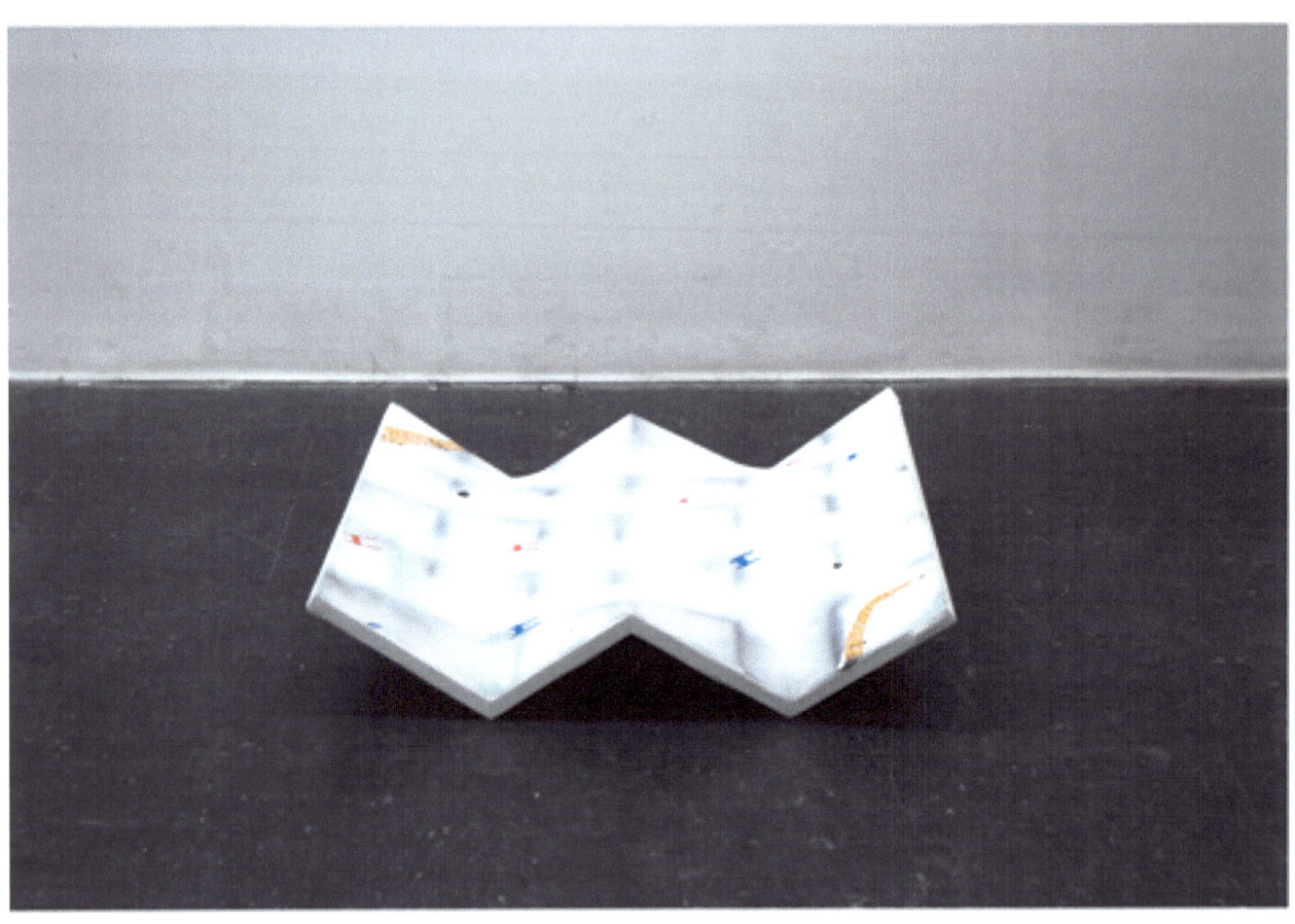

(even though that shouldn't be cheesy and its only my modern sensibilities telling me being sincere is cliche). I don't know.... ideas sex, humor what else is there? maybe i'll eventually get around to doing death but not yet.

How are you referencing the history of abstract painting, or challenging it, or does that even matter?

There is nothing more quintessential about the history of abstract painting.... than challenging the history of painting. So the irony of radicality is that if you rebel against the avant-garde of yesteryear... you are really embodying their spirit. I think there is no way out of this mindset which just heads towards nihilism, in painting that is embodied by market driven crapstraction and impotent deconstructions of painting. Smashing apart your LEGO building is really fun, but so is building it in a strange new way, and what definitely isn't fun or meaningful is smashing your already destroyed pile of LEGO rubble. Painting and aesthetics aren't some distant or dead thing to me like they were to my professors. I think the post-history free for all is over, and was hypocritcally very historical. I think stylistically the eclecticism of the younger generation of painters is not the post-

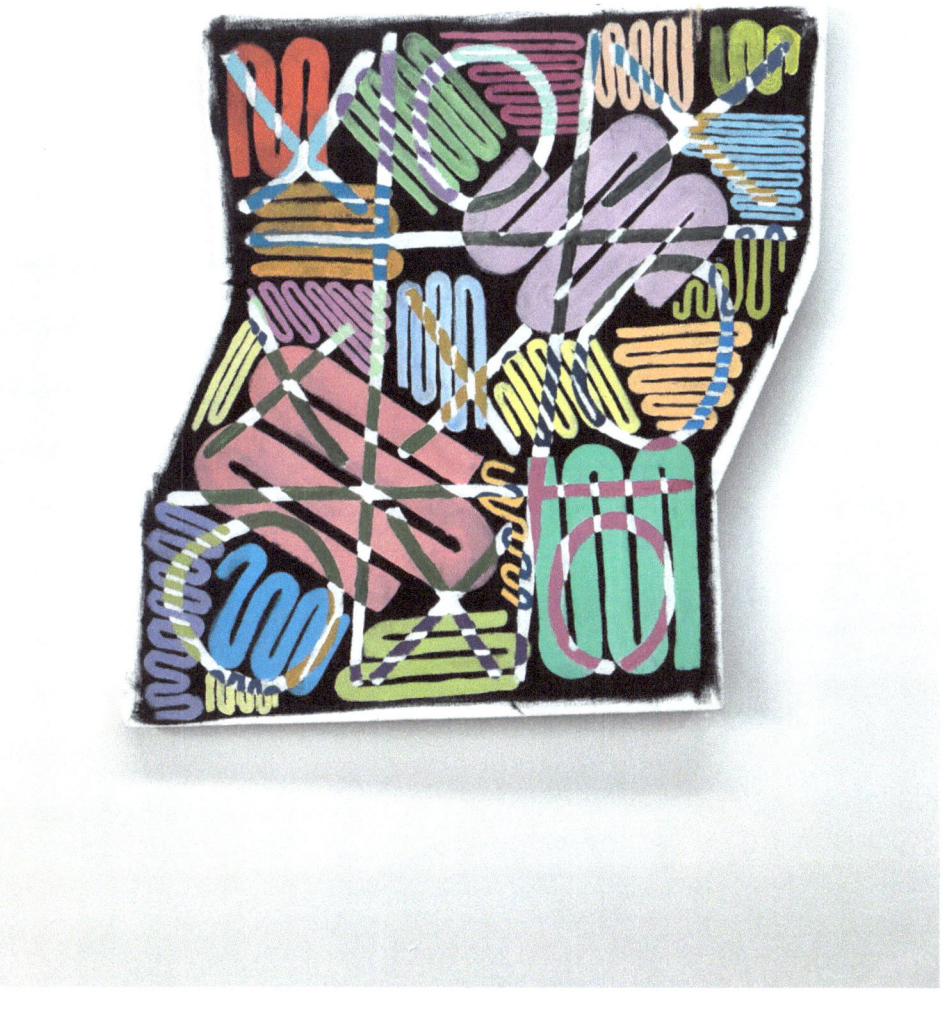

historical, cherry-picking, cool and distant meaninglessness of post modernism, like the eclecticism of older painters. I think the diversity of styles in young painters is baroque, meaningful and sincere. We all challenge and don't challenge various different histories. Something about the phrase "history of (abstract) painting" feels stilted and dead. I'm playing the game of (abstract) painting, I can walk through a museum and see how others played painting, what it meant to them etc.

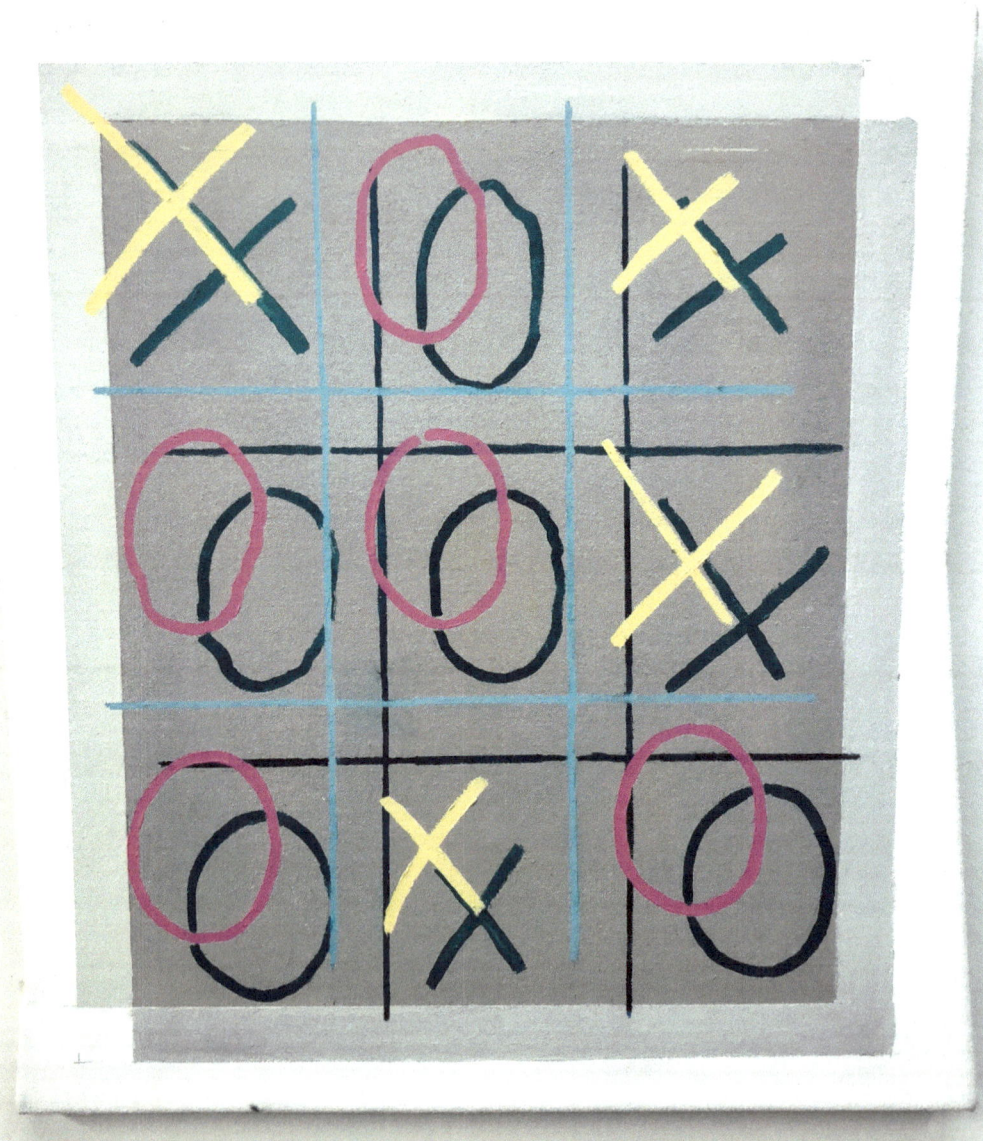

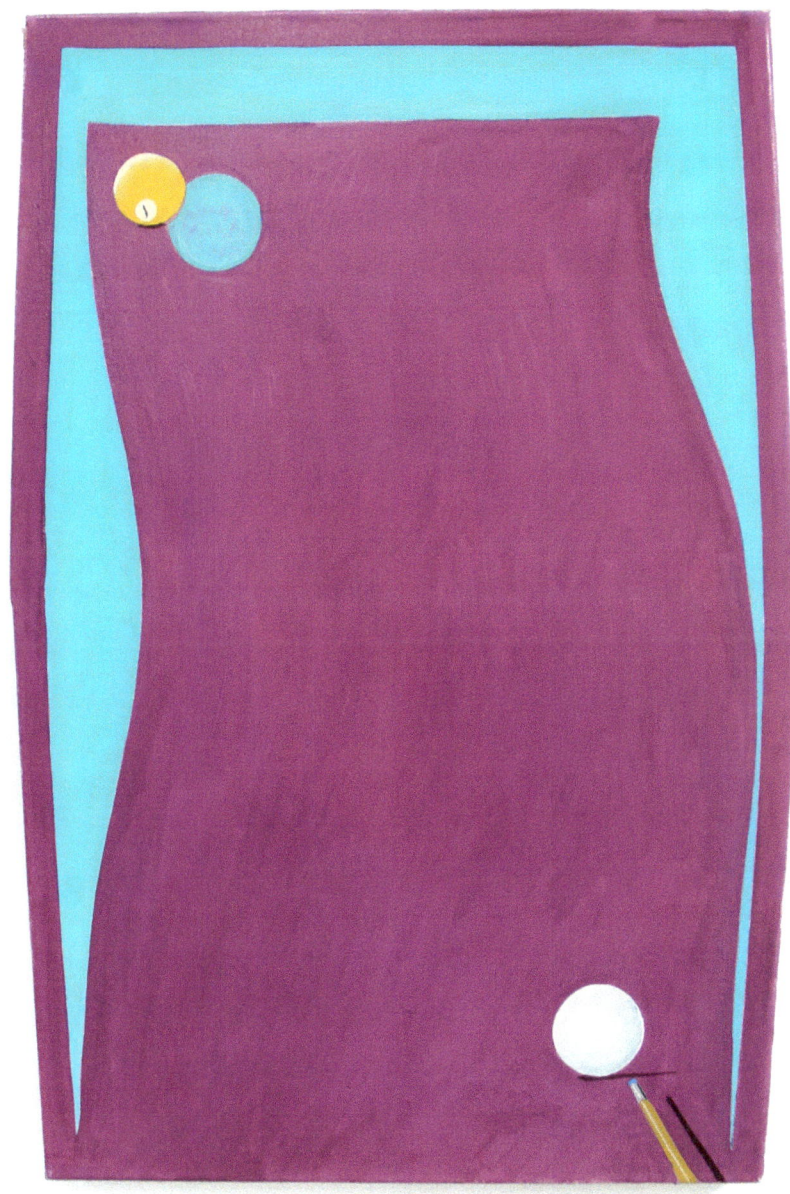

Is the materiality of paint or the action of painting important to your work? Could the work being made and any other medium?

Paint is a mix color and stuff. Light waves and matter. There is nothing really unique about it. I guess we build associations with it but I'm not a medium essentialist. Doing things by hang generally feels better than by machine. Oil paint generally has better color and definitely better mixing capabilities. I use caulk sometimes but I use it like paint so...

Paints physicality works better for certain ideas, photography is better for others, crayons are better for others, etc. I think the conventions of painting, its internal language and its physical structure have developed overtime to express subjectivity in an objective form.

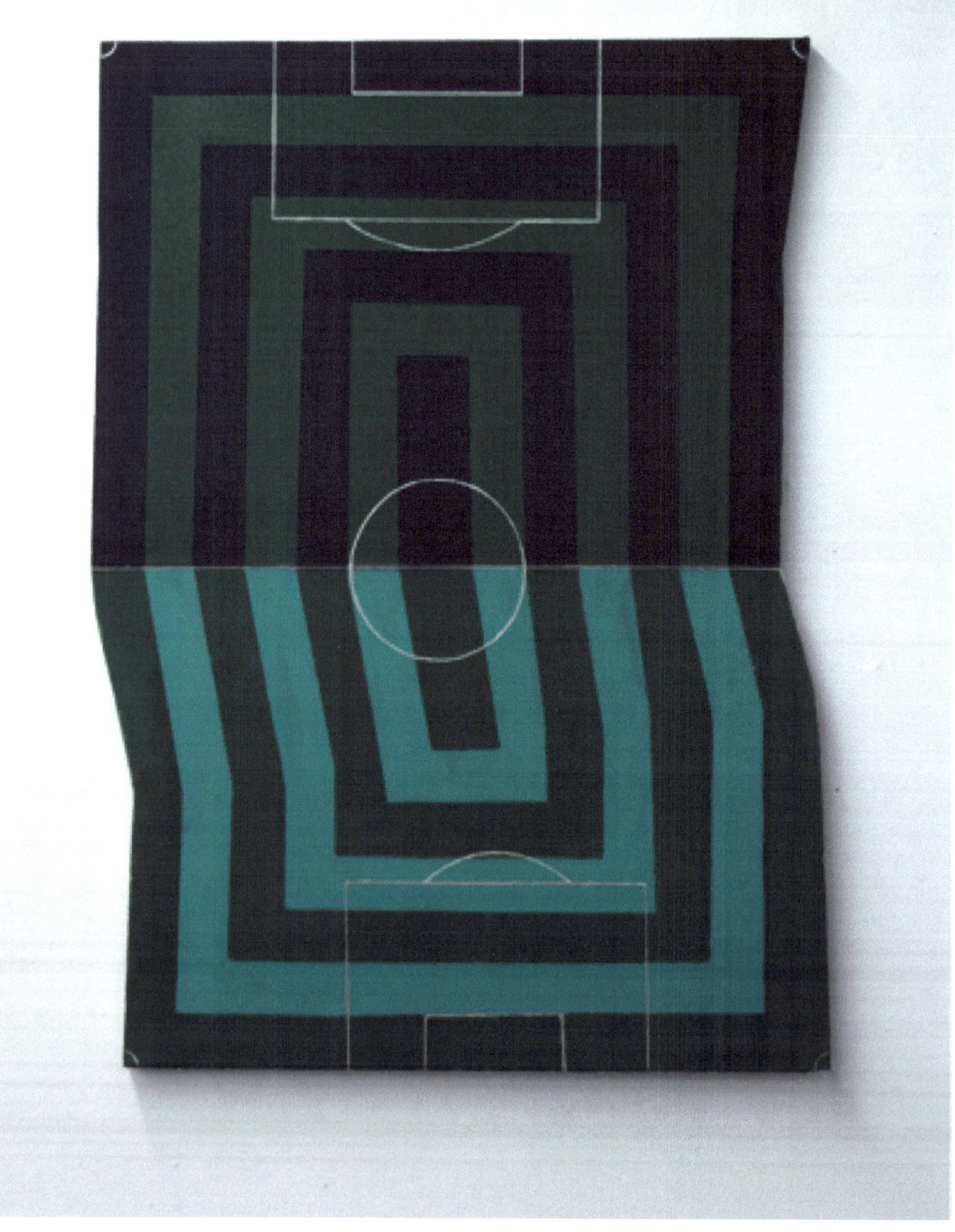

international contemporary art

WERKS

Issue 1 is still available online and in select stores!

issue 01 / spring 2018

www.ingramcontent.com/pod-product-compliance
Lightning Source LLC
Chambersburg PA
CBHW051050180526
45172CB00002B/583